I0814533

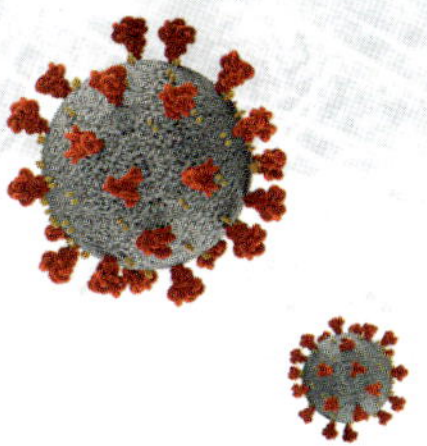

COVID-19 VACCINES AND TREATMENTS

BY CARLA MOONEY

CONTENT CONSULTANT
Kenneth A. Stapleford, PhD
Assistant Professor
Department of Microbiology
New York University Grossman School of Medicine

Essential Library
An Imprint of Abdo Publishing
abdobooks.com

ABDOBOOKS.COM

Printed in the United States of America, North Mankato, Minnesota.
052022
092022

Cover Photo: Prostock Studio/Alamy
Interior Photos: Shutterstock Images, 4, 13, 21, 41, 70; Mark Lennihan/Pool/AP Images, 7; Feature China/Future Publishing/Getty Images, 14; James Gathany/Brian Judd/CDC, 18; CDC, 24; Silvio Avila/Getty Images News/Getty Images, 27; Michele Eve Sandberg/Sipa USA/AP Images, 31; Donato Fasano/Getty Images News/Getty Images, 37; Ted S. Warren/AP Images, 38; Taimy Alvarez/AP Images, 45; Saul Loeb/Pool/AP Images, 48; Prostock Studio/Shutterstock Images, 50; Kateryna Kon/Shutterstock Images, 56; Red Line Editorial, 58, 88; Eric Lee/Bloomberg/Getty Images, 60; Jae C. Hong/AP Images, 63; Michael Nagle/Xinhua News Agency/Getty Images, 66; Luka Dakskobler/SOPA Images/Light Rocket/Getty Images, 78; Stuart Monk/Shutterstock Images, 80; Brian Inganga/AP Images, 86; Ringo H. W. Chiu/AP Images, 90; Alexi Rosenfeld/Getty Images Entertainment/Getty Images, 94; Jerome Delay/AP Images, 96

Editor: Marie Pearson
Designer: Becky Daum

Library of Congress Control Number: 2021951383
Publisher's Cataloging-in-Publication Data
Names: Mooney, Carla, author.
Title: Covid-19 vaccines and treatments / by Carla Mooney
Description: Minneapolis, Minnesota : Abdo Publishing, 2023 | Series: Fighting covid-19 | Includes online resources and index.
Identifiers: ISBN 9781532198007 (lib. bdg.) | ISBN 9781098271657 (ebook)
Subjects: LCSH: COVID-19 (Disease)--Juvenile literature. | Communicable diseases--Vaccination--Juvenile literature. | Vaccine mandates--Juvenile literature. | Therapeutics--Juvenile literature. | Civilization, Modern--21st century--Juvenile literature. | United States--History--Juvenile literature.
Classification: DDC 614.592--dc23

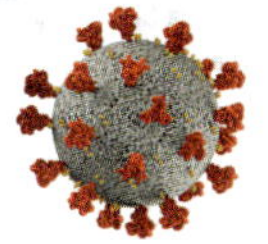
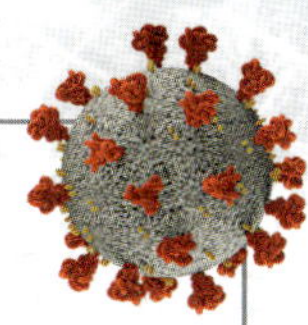
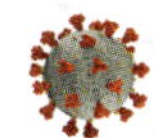

CONTENTS

PAA166078
Pfizer-BioNTech COVID
After dilution, vial contains 6
For intramuscular use. Contains
For use under Emergency Use
DILUTE BEFORE USE. Discard
dilution when stored at 2 to 25
Dilution date and time:

CHAPTER ONE

A SHOT HEARD AROUND THE WORLD

On November 9, 2020, American biotechnology company Pfizer and its partner BioNTech, a German biotechnology company, made an announcement. They said that they had successfully developed an effective vaccine against coronavirus disease 2019 (COVID-19), the illness caused by the severe acute respiratory syndrome coronavirus 2 (SARS-CoV-2), a virus that had been discovered less than a year prior. In clinical trials, Pfizer's vaccine was more than 90 percent effective in preventing COVID-19.[1] The announcement signaled a significant step in fighting the COVID-19 pandemic, which had infected and killed millions of people worldwide since the time of its first recorded cases in December 2019.

Pfizer and BioNTech's announcement about their vaccine brought hope to many people that COVID-19 would no longer be as dangerous of a disease.

On December 11, 2020, the US Food and Drug Administration (FDA) issued an emergency use authorization (EUA) to allow the Pfizer-BioNTech COVID-19 vaccine to be used in the United States. FDA commissioner Stephen M. Hahn said, "The tireless work to develop a new vaccine to prevent this novel, serious, and life-threatening disease in an expedited timeframe after its emergence is a true testament to scientific innovation and public-private collaboration worldwide."[2]

EMERGENCY USE AUTHORIZATION

During the COVID-19 pandemic, the FDA issued several EUAs for tests, treatments, and vaccines. An EUA is used during a declared emergency, such as a pandemic, when the FDA might not have all the data it usually gathers and analyzes before approving a drug, test, or device. If there is enough evidence to show the FDA that a treatment or test benefits patients, then the agency can issue an EUA so that it can be used before final approval.

Within days, the first Americans received the vaccine shot as it was offered to the public for the first time. At the Long Island Jewish Medical Center in Queens, New York City, officials asked for staff volunteers to receive the first doses of the COVID-19 vaccine. Sandra Lindsay, the director of critical care nursing, raised her hand to get the vaccine. Since the pandemic, 52-year-old Lindsay had led a team of critical care nurses that cared for very sick COVID-19 patients. Lindsay worked on the floor with her nurses, lending a hand to rotate patients on their beds, bathe them, and take care of their needs. The amount of sickness and suffering she witnessed firsthand was staggering. "Some days, I don't know how I got through

Sandra Lindsay received the first COVID-19 vaccine available to the US public.

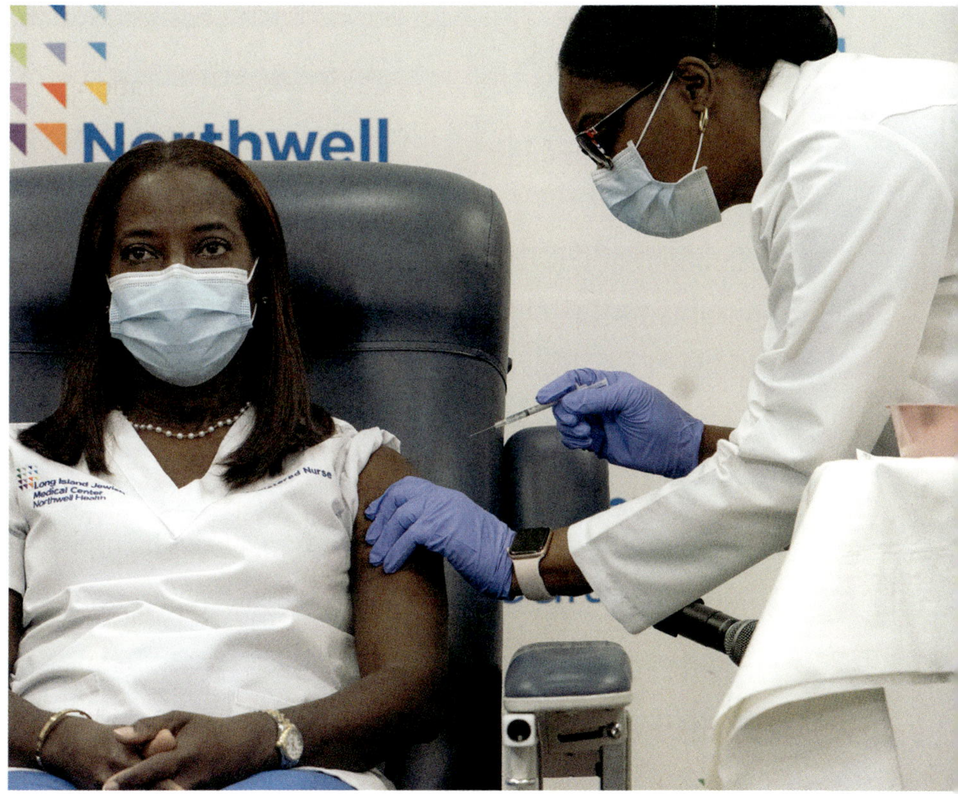

it," she said. Lindsay added, "Some days, I didn't know how I got home, but I knew I had to rest and get ready to come back and do it again. Because I did not want to leave my team to do it alone."[3]

Around 9:20 a.m. on Monday, December 14, 2020, Lindsay got the shot. Her vaccination was televised live on CNN and streamed into a news conference held by New York governor Andrew Cuomo. New York state officials declared Lindsay the first person in the United States to get a COVID-19 vaccine. "It feels surreal," Lindsay said. "It is a huge sense of relief for me, and hope." She urged others to get vaccinated when it was their turn. "The alternative and what I have seen and experienced is far worse," she said. "So it's important that everyone pulls together to take the vaccine, not only to

> "I have no doubt we'll emerge stronger from this virus than we were before. . . . The coronavirus pandemic will change forever the way we conduct scientific investigations in this country and around the world."[4]
>
> *—Moshe Arditi, academic director of Pediatric Infectious Diseases and Immunology at Cedars-Sinai Medical Center in Los Angeles, California*

protect themselves but also to protect everyone they will come into contact with."[5]

A NEW VIRUS EMERGES

In December 2019, several people in Wuhan, China, experienced flu-like symptoms, including shortness of breath and fever. By the end of December, the World Health Organization (WHO) office in China learned of several cases of pneumonia from an unknown cause centered in Wuhan. By January 7, 2020, Chinese officials had identified a novel, or new, coronavirus as the cause of the illness outbreak. On January 31, 2020, Alex Azar, the secretary of the US Department of Health and Human Services (HHS), declared the novel coronavirus a public health emergency. Through February 2020, public health officials struggled to understand how the virus spread, how to contain it, and how to treat it. Countries that experienced early outbreaks like China and Italy imposed lockdowns on their citizens to limit the virus's spread. COVID-19 cases spread to more countries, and on March 11, 2020, the WHO declared COVID-19 a pandemic.

In the United States, the first cases of COVID-19 appeared in early 2020. On March 13, President Donald

SPREADING WORLDWIDE

The SARS-CoV-2 virus became a pandemic because of its ability to quickly spread far and wide. Several factors affect how far and how quickly a disease can spread. One of the most important factors is how easily the disease can be transmitted from one person to another. A second factor is the movement of people from one area of the world to another. When people travel on airplanes, they can spread disease to other regions around the globe in hours. A local outbreak becomes a global pandemic.

Trump declared a national emergency. Within a few days, the country began to shut down to slow the spread of the virus. Many other countries did the same. At first, several countries closed their borders, schools, and businesses. They instituted lockdowns and ordered citizens to stay at home for weeks or months at a time. When communities began to reopen, many governments required citizens to wear masks and practice social distancing, restricted the operation of schools and some businesses, and limited the size of public and private gatherings.

The virus that forced millions of people to stay home for months was a new type of coronavirus. It was highly contagious and spread primarily through saliva or nasal discharge droplets when an infected person spoke, sneezed, or coughed. Most who contracted the virus experienced mild to moderate symptoms, including cough, fever, shortness of breath, body aches, sore throat, loss of taste or smell, gastrointestinal distress, headache, and congestion. However, many others became severely ill with COVID-19, the disease caused by the virus. By April 2022, according to the Johns Hopkins Coronavirus Resource Center, nearly 6.2 million people worldwide had died of COVID-19.[6]

Over the course of the pandemic, infection rates and COVID-19 hospitalizations rose and fell in waves. In many places, businesses that had reopened found it necessary to close again. Schools that had started bringing students back into the classroom

1918 INFLUENZA PANDEMIC

In 1918, an influenza pandemic sickened and killed millions of people worldwide. The pandemic was caused by an influenza virus that spread around the world during 1918 and 1919. About 500 million people, one-third of the world's population, were infected with the virus. An estimated 50 million people died. In the United States, the death toll was about 675,000.[7] While the SARS-CoV-2 virus was most serious for the elderly, the 1918 influenza virus targeted younger people. At the time, there was no vaccine to protect against the virus. There were also no antibiotics to treat secondary infections. Measures such as isolation, quarantine, and limited public gatherings were put in place to limit the spread of the virus.

returned to online learning. People longed for things to return to the pre-pandemic normal.

THE NEED FOR A VACCINE

To slow the spread of the novel coronavirus that caused COVID-19, some people worldwide took public health measures to limit exposure and infection. When some people learned they had been in close contact with a person who had COVID-19, they quarantined at home. If they tested positive for the virus, they isolated themselves from people who were not sick to prevent further spread. In public settings, people wore masks and practiced social distancing, meaning they kept at least six feet (1.8 m) between themselves and people from other households, to slow the virus's spread. These measures helped temporarily, but they were not long-term solutions. The development of a COVID-19 vaccine was desperately needed to protect health worldwide.

Scientists around the world got to work on developing vaccines for COVID-19. Vaccines typically take years to develop. Creating a vaccine in less than a year would be a monumental accomplishment. Researchers shared their data with other scientists. This worldwide cooperation

Drive-in COVID-19 testing facilities sprang up early in the pandemic to help people determine whether they needed to isolate from others to prevent spreading the disease.

allowed labs to fast-track research and clinical trials. The race against time to develop a COVID-19 vaccine had begun.

CHAPTER TWO

A HIGHLY CONTAGIOUS VIRUS

On January 7, 2020, Chinese researchers announced that they had identified the virus causing the mysterious outbreak in Wuhan that had sickened dozens of people. It was a new strain of coronavirus, the family of viruses that causes the common cold as well as illnesses such as severe acute respiratory syndrome (SARS) and Middle East respiratory syndrome (MERS). Chinese researchers performed laboratory tests on swab samples from sick patients and eliminated known coronaviruses and other known common respiratory pathogens.

When studying the samples, the researchers isolated what appeared to be a new coronavirus. They obtained a genome sequence, which identified the complete genetic code of the virus and confirmed that it was a novel coronavirus. The WHO said in a statement

The Chinese government set up some temporary walls in Wuhan, China, in March 2020 to try to contain the spread of the new virus by limiting where people in areas with infection outbreaks could go.

two days after the discovery, "According to Chinese authorities, the virus in question can cause severe illness in some patients and does not transmit readily between people."[1] On February 11, 2020, scientists announced the name of the new virus: SARS-CoV-2. Much still needed to be learned about this new virus.

SARS AND MERS

SARS and MERS are viral respiratory diseases caused by coronaviruses. SARS was first identified in February 2003 in China. Like influenza and the common cold, SARS is caused by an airborne virus that spreads through tiny respiratory droplets. It can also be spread by touching surfaces touched by an infected person. Nearly 10 percent of SARS cases are fatal.[2] Since 2004, there have been no known cases of SARS reported worldwide.

First reported in Saudi Arabia in 2012, MERS is a severe illness that causes fever, cough, and shortness of breath. It is transmitted when another person inhales respiratory droplets from an infected person nearby. However, MERS is not easily spread from person to person. Most cases of spread occur when a person becomes infected after caring for or living with an infected person. According to the CDC, 30 to 40 percent of MERS cases are fatal.[3]

TRANSMISSION AND PREVENTION

At first, scientists did not believe SARS-CoV-2 spread through human-to-human contact, and China had reported no infections among health-care workers treating patients or family members exposed to sick patients. However, it soon became clear that the SARS-CoV-2 virus spread between people through contact transmission and droplet transmission. Contact transmission occurs when a person is in direct contact with an infected person or touches a surface that is contaminated with virus particles. Droplet transmission happens when an infected person breathes, speaks, sings, coughs, or sneezes. They expel virus particles into the air and infect a nearby person.

After the discovery of these transmission methods, people around the world cleaned and disinfected surfaces in an effort to prevent contact transmission. Mask mandates, which required people to wear masks in public settings, and social distancing guidelines attempted to limit the number of infectious particles in the air and

GENOME SEQUENCING

A genome is the complete genetic code of an organism. An organism's genetic code is a set of instructions that holds all the information necessary to develop, grow, and stay alive. Every organism, including a virus, has a unique genome. When scientists sequence an organism's genome, they determine the order of the chemicals in the molecules that make up the organism's genetic code. Whole-genome sequencing can provide detailed data for identifying disease outbreaks like those caused by SARS-CoV-2.

Sneezing sends saliva into the air. If a person is infected with a virus, the virus can be trapped in the saliva too.

the number of people in close contact with an infected person, preventing droplet transmission.

At first, many experts believed it was unlikely that SARS-CoV-2 could be an airborne virus. While larger particles often fall to the ground or nearby surfaces within a few seconds, airborne transmission happens when smaller particles linger in the air and accumulate in indoor spaces. However, evidence began to mount that respiratory particles were small enough to remain

> **"This is a reality check for every government on the planet: Wake up. Get ready. This virus may be on its way and you need to be ready."[4]**
>
> *—Mike Ryan, executive director of the WHO's health emergencies program, on February 28, 2020, about the potential risk of the new coronavirus*

suspended in the air for long periods and travel farther, exposing more people to infection. Eventually, the world came to acknowledge that SARS-CoV-2 was airborne. Understanding transmission was key to preventing illness. At a time when little was known about how to treat COVID-19, prevention was all the more important.

On February 11, 2020, the WHO announced the name of the disease caused by the SARS-CoV-2 virus: COVID-19. The US Centers for Disease Control and Prevention (CDC) developed a laboratory test to identify SARS-CoV-2 from respiratory specimens. This would allow medical authorities to diagnose and track infections. The first test was released in February 2020.

AIRBORNE SPREAD

In July 2020, more than 200 scientists published a statement urging the international community to recognize the potential for airborne spread of SARS-CoV-2 and called for additional precautions to limit airborne transmission. Lidia Morawska and Donald K. Milton, the statement's authors, wrote, "We are concerned that the lack of recognition of the risk of airborne transmission of COVID-19 and the lack of clear recommendations on the control measures against the airborne virus will have significant consequences: people may think that they are fully protected by adhering to the current recommendations, but in fact, additional airborne interventions are needed for further reduction of infection risk."[5]

ATTACKING THE BODY

Scientists also scrambled to learn more about how the virus affected the body. Infected patients displayed a range of symptoms. For some people, the COVID-19 illness and its symptoms were mild, and some infected people were asymptomatic, showing no symptoms. However, for others, COVID-19 could be very serious and life-threatening.

Like other respiratory viruses, SARS-CoV-2 enters the body through the nose, mouth, or eyes. Once it enters the body, the virus attacks healthy cells. It takes over these cells and uses them to replicate, or make more virus particles. When the cell becomes full of virus particles, it splits open and releases them. The cell dies, and the virus particles move throughout the body and infect more cells.

As the virus attacks cells, the body's immune system tries to mount a counterattack on the invader. The immune system creates inflammation, making it more difficult for the virus to replicate. The immune system produces many symptoms, such as fever and a cough. When the virus travels through the lungs, the immune system can trigger inflammation in the lungs, leading to breathing trouble and pneumonia.

For many people with mild cases of COVID-19, symptoms lessen after several days. Although people might have some lingering symptoms, such as a cough or loss of taste or smell, most feel much better in a few weeks. Severe cases often occur when the virus multiplies in the lungs and causes inflammation that affects breathing.

Fluid buildup and inflammation in the lungs can trigger fluid to leak into the tiny air sacs in the lungs. When this occurs, a person may develop a critical condition called acute respiratory distress

Doctors typically take chest X-rays to diagnose pneumonia.

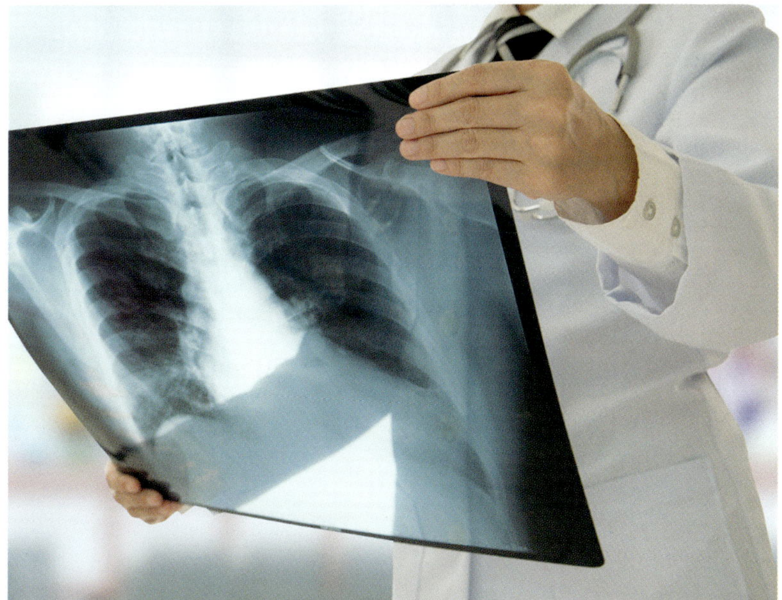

syndrome (ARDS). Normally when a person inhales air, oxygen in the air moves into the lungs. Tiny air sacs in the lungs called alveoli exchange gases with tiny blood vessels called capillaries. Oxygen from the air is transferred to the bloodstream and carried throughout the body.

With ARDS, the lungs struggle to move oxygen from the air to the bloodstream. As a result, the body's organs cannot get the oxygen they need. A healthy person has a blood oxygen level of 95 percent or higher. When the blood oxygen level drops to 88 percent or lower, a person generally needs supplementary oxygen. For seriously ill COVID-19 patients, blood oxygen levels fall into the 60 to 70 percent range.[6] Without enough oxygen, the body's organs start to shut down.

Some patients experienced further complications from COVID-19. The longer the body fights the infection, the more tired it becomes, weakening organs. The patient becomes more susceptible to pneumonia and other infections in this weakened state. Some patients develop very low blood pressure, which can cause even more problems, including kidney failure. If the kidneys begin to fail, the body cannot effectively filter waste and excess fluid from the blood. The virus can also weaken the heart, which can be fatal, especially in people with pre-existing heart conditions. People who develop severe cases of COVID-19 are more likely to experience permanent scarring of the lungs. "It's too early to know what the long-term effects of the coronavirus are going to be," Heather Strah, a pulmonary medicine and critical care specialist, said. "We think the majority of people who come off the ventilator and recover will be able to return to a relatively normal life. A small minority of patients may need specialized medical care, like oxygen or dialysis, for the rest of their lives."[7]

FIRST US PATIENT

In January 2020, a 35-year-old man fell ill. He had just returned to Washington State from a trip to Wuhan. While in Wuhan, the man had not visited the seafood market that experts believed was the source of the new coronavirus outbreak. After four days of coughing and vomiting, the man called a local urgent care clinic for advice on January 19. The clinic ran several tests on the man but did not find anything. They gave him an N95 mask and told him to go home and quarantine. Meanwhile, the clinic overnight shipped the man's nasal swab to the CDC headquarters in Atlanta, Georgia. The next day, the test results came back. The man was the first confirmed patient in the United States to be infected with the new virus.

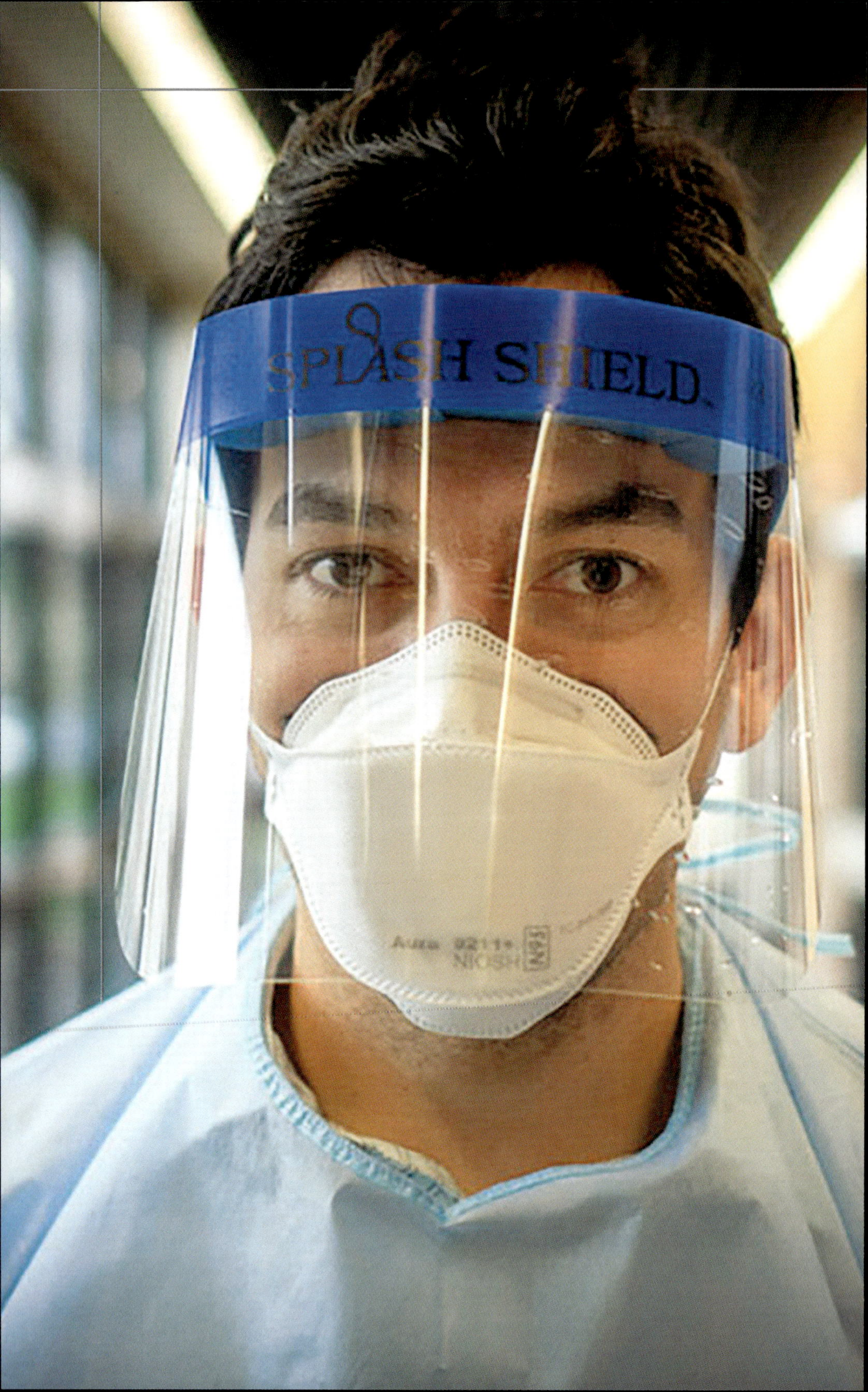
SPLASH SHIELD

CHAPTER THREE

TREATING COVID-19

For some, COVID-19 becomes severe enough that they need hospital care. By the time they reach the hospital, most patients have already been fighting COVID-19 for at least a week. During this time, the virus has spread throughout the body. The immune system is at a dangerous point as it ramps up its attack against the virus. Although the immune system's attack targets the virus, it can also cause significant damage to the body and its organs. In the sickest COVID-19 patients, this damage can lead to serious illness and death.

Early in the pandemic, doctors and nurses around the world prepared to treat a disease they had never seen before. In February 2020, infectious disease doctor Norio Ohmagari in Tokyo, Japan, turned to a treatment plan that he knew for the related coronavirus that causes MERS. "Honestly, we were not quite sure what we could do," he said.[1]

Health-care workers did their best to protect themselves from infection as hospitals filled with COVID-19 patients.

Hospital staff struggled to keep up with a disease that could turn serious quickly, sending patients to intensive care units (ICUs) without warning. Doctors tried to understand why some patients died while others recovered. "As physicians, we always see death. That's part of our training, but what was different now was that we were dealing with a new disease. There were patients who were dying. We felt—I hate to use the word—helpless," said Adarsh Bhimraj, a doctor at the Cleveland Clinic.[2]

Typically, doctors rely on results from large clinical trials to guide treatment decisions. But this kind of data was not available at the time. Most of the early efforts to treat COVID-19 patients focused on improving breathing and oxygen levels. If a person's blood oxygen level dipped below 94 percent, the first treatment was often oxygen delivered through a mask or nasal prongs.[3]

Many patients with ARDS were treated in hospital ICUs and needed help breathing from a ventilator for two to three weeks or longer. A ventilator is a machine that pumps air, often with extra oxygen, into a patient's airways when the patient cannot breathe adequately without help. Because ventilators are very uncomfortable, patients are usually sedated. By the spring of 2020, many doctors had started flipping ventilator patients from their backs to their stomachs for up to 16 hours per day.[4] Placing the sickest patients on their stomachs is called prone positioning and helps increase the amount of oxygen getting into their lungs and blood.

When patients on ventilators lie on their backs, the heart and other organs push down on the lungs. Prone position can reduce this pressure, allowing more oxygen to circulate in the lungs.

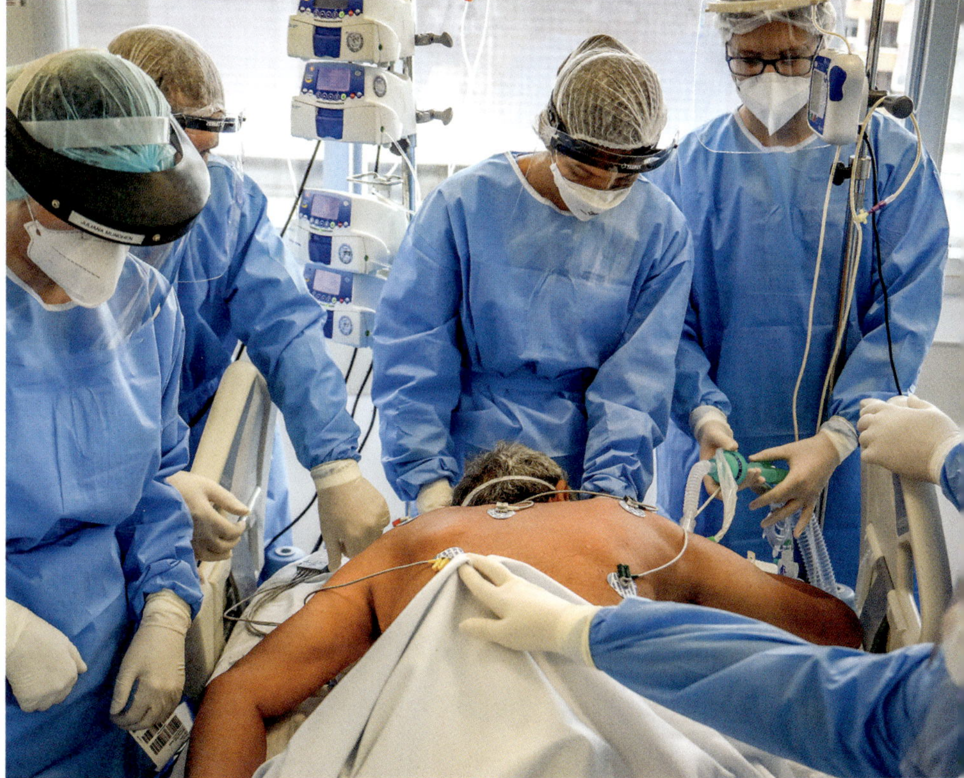

DRUGS

As doctors searched for ways to save their patients, they turned to unproven drugs such as hydroxychloroquine, which is used against the disease malaria. Early in the outbreak, French doctors reported that hydroxychloroquine appeared to save lives in COVID-19 patients. Prescriptions for the medication soared in March 2020. However, later studies determined that hydroxychloroquine accelerated death in some patients.

The HIV drugs lopinavir and ritonavir appeared to be promising treatments when prescribed together. However, the drug combination was later found to have little effect on saving lives for COVID-19 patients. Because little was known about the disease in the early months of the pandemic, many COVID-19 patients received treatments that did not work and, in some cases, did more harm than good.

As doctors learned more, treatment guidelines changed as quickly as they were made. "Every time I take care of a COVID patient . . . I have to sit down and go, 'OK, what are we doing now?'" said Meghan Lane-Fall, a critical care physician in Philadelphia, Pennsylvania.[5]

Slowly, things began to change. With each patient, doctors learned more. They started to catch early warning signs that a patient may experience a severe case and learned to intervene earlier and more effectively.

Remdesivir was a drug used early on that ended up showing some promise. The antiviral medication was initially developed to treat the Ebola and hepatitis C viruses. It is given intravenously, meaning it's injected in the bloodstream, over several days. In lab testing, remdesivir showed an ability to inhibit the SARS-CoV-2 virus. An international trial sponsored by the National Institutes of Health (NIH) in 2020 reported that using the medication shortened hospital stays by several days. It appeared most beneficial for patients who needed

RISK FACTORS FOR SEVERE DISEASE

Some people are at greater risk than others for developing severe COVID-19. One of the most significant risk factors is age. Those age 85 or older have the greatest risk of severe disease. In the United States, more than 80 percent of COVID-19 deaths have occurred in people age 65 and older.[6] In addition, some pre-existing health conditions can increase the risk for severe disease. These include heart and lung conditions, weakened immune systems, cancer, certain blood disorders, chronic kidney or liver conditions, obesity, and diabetes.

supplemental oxygen but did not yet need to be in the ICU or on a ventilator. In May 2020, the FDA issued an EUA that made remdesivir available to hospitalized patients. In October 2020, the FDA fully approved the drug to treat all hospitalized patients with COVID-19. However, a larger trial, sponsored by the WHO that same month, found no significant change in hospital stay or death for COVID-19 patients taking remdesivir. But because the medication has few side effects, it remained a standard COVID-19 therapy in most hospitals in the United States in 2022.

CONVALESCENT BLOOD PLASMA THERAPY

Some treatments used the immune system for inspiration. When a person becomes infected with a virus and then recovers, the immune system produces antibodies to fight the virus in the future. Convalescent plasma therapy gives COVID-19 patients a transfusion of blood plasma from a person who has recovered from the disease. The hope is that the antibodies in the donor's plasma will help the patient fight the virus.

Between April 2020 and November 2021, doctors treated more than 500,000 COVID-19 patients with

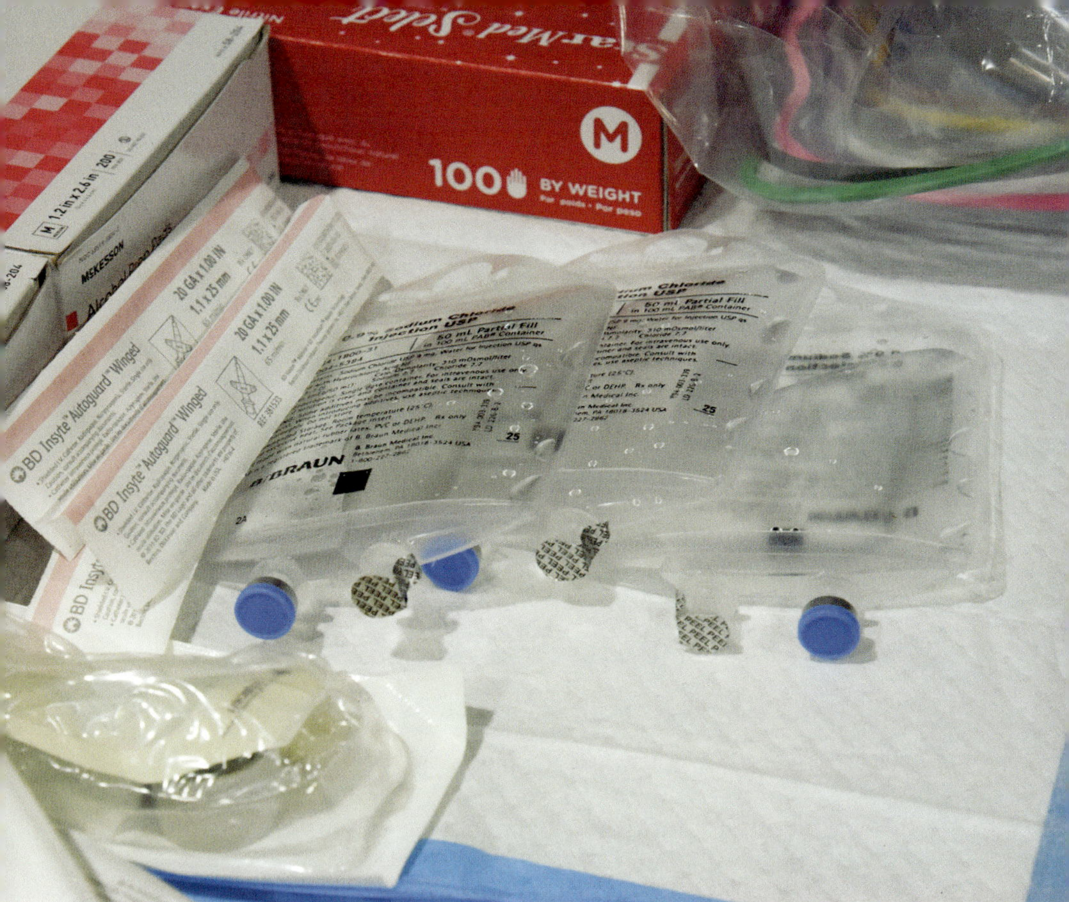

Monoclonal antibodies are given through an intravenous (IV) infusion.

convalescent plasma therapy. However, the use of this treatment declined in 2021 as several trials returned inconsistent results. In December 2021, the WHO recommended against using convalescent plasma to treat COVID-19.

MONOCLONAL ANTIBODIES

Treatment of COVID-19 with monoclonal antibodies also showed promise. Monoclonal antibodies are laboratory-created proteins that mimic the body's immune response. They are designed to block the virus from attaching to cells. In November 2020, the FDA issued an EUA for the first monoclonal antibodies to treat COVID-19.

Early evidence suggested that monoclonal antibodies could reduce the chances of hospitalization in people at risk of severe disease if they were given early in the illness. One study reported in March 2021 that antibodies reduced hospitalization or death among participants by 85 percent. In another trial, a cocktail of two antibodies decreased the risk of hospitalization and death by 87 percent.[7] Monoclonal antibodies can be a key therapy for immunosuppressed patients who cannot make adequate antibodies themselves.

In some cases, access could be a problem with monoclonal antibodies. Because the treatment needed to be given in a hospital, patients who could benefit from the treatment may not have received it because they could not get to a hospital that had it. Also, monoclonal antibodies appeared to be most effective when given in the first three or four days of showing symptoms. Patients who did not have access to the medication during that short window may not have received the treatment.

IMMUNOSUPPRESSANT MEDICATIONS

In the sickest COVID-19 patients, the immune system ramps up to attack the invading virus. But the immune system's attack also damages the body and its organs. Some immune-suppressing medications proved helpful when a patient reached this serious stage of the disease. Immunosuppressant drugs reduce the strength of the body's immune system. They are often used in transplant patients to prevent the body from rejecting a transplanted organ or to treat patients with autoimmune disorders, such as lupus, where the body's immune system attacks itself.

One such immunosuppressant

OUTPATIENT CARE

Most people who develop COVID-19 can receive outpatient care and recover at home. For mild to moderate cases of COVID-19, doctors give patients the same advice they offer for the flu and other viruses: rest, drink fluids, and take acetaminophen for pain and fever. However, COVID-19 can turn bad very quickly. To monitor blood oxygen levels, which can indicate severe disease, many doctors recommend that patients use pulse oximeters at home to detect falling blood oxygen levels and seek help quickly.

medication is dexamethasone, a cheap and common steroid. In the United Kingdom, tens of thousands of hospitalized patients participated in a trial that included dexamethasone as a potential COVID-19 treatment. For the sickest patients on ventilators, dexamethasone had promising results. Patients who received the steroid had a mortality rate of 29 percent by 28 days after admission. In comparison, patients who did not receive the steroid had a mortality rate of 41 percent.[8] In early 2021, the trial found that tocilizumab, an anti-inflammatory drug approved to treat rheumatoid arthritis, improved survival in the sickest patients.

ANTICOAGULANTS

Some COVID-19 patients experience blood clots that can cause life-threatening heart attacks, strokes, and more if left untreated. For patients with severe disease, doctors perform blood tests to determine the activity of their blood-clotting systems. Patients with active clotting systems are at a higher risk of developing clots. These patients can take anticoagulant medications to prevent the formation of blood clots. However, because ICU patients are also at risk of bleeding due to illness or invasive treatments, doctors must weigh the benefits and risks of anticoagulant medications in COVID-19 patients. Patients with less active clotting systems and a lower risk of blood clots may do well on alternative treatments such as compression socks or low-dose injections of blood thinners.

ADVANCEMENTS

Beyond drugs, doctors improved their intensive care practices. Ventilators can cause long-term lung injury. With time, doctors experimented with less invasive ways to provide oxygen. For example, doctors instructed patients struggling to breathe to rest on their stomachs. This prone position reduces compression on the lungs caused by the heart and abdominal organs and improves gas exchange in the lungs. It can also improve heart function and help fluids drain better from the lungs.

While much progress was made in treating COVID-19, people continued to die from the disease. In 2021, most of the treatments being used were existing therapies repurposed to fight COVID-19. Researchers

ANTIVIRAL MEDICATIONS

Antiviral medications are drugs developed to treat diseases caused by a virus. A virus is a tiny infectious pathogen that grows and multiplies inside an organism's living cells. A virus has receptors that attach to a healthy host cell. Once the virus is attached to a host cell, it can enter the cell and make copies of itself. The host cell dies, and the virus spreads to other healthy cells. Antiviral medications work primarily by blocking the ability of the virus to replicate inside a host cell. Some antiviral medications also lessen the amount of virus (the viral load) in the body and strengthen the immune system to fight the virus. Antiviral medications can shorten an illness and reduce complications in some people.

worked on developing new antiviral medications specifically designed to treat the disease and stop the virus from replicating before a devastating immune response occurred.

In November 2021, Pfizer announced that its new antiviral medication for treating COVID-19, Paxlovid, was highly effective at preventing severe illness in high-risk people. When given within three days after symptoms begin, Paxlovid decreased the risk of hospitalization or death by 89 percent.[9] Annaliesa Anderson, a Pfizer executive who led the drug's development, said she hoped the drug could "have a big impact on helping all our lives go back to normal again and seeing the end of the pandemic."[10] In December 2021, the FDA granted an EUA for the Pfizer medication.

> "I've now seen hundreds of people with COVID-19. It's an awful disease. What motivates me is to try to get them back to their loved ones."[11]
>
> —*George Diaz, an infectious diseases specialist in Everett, Washington*

Paxlovid is one of a new class of easy-to-use pills that have the potential to reduce COVID-19 hospitalizations

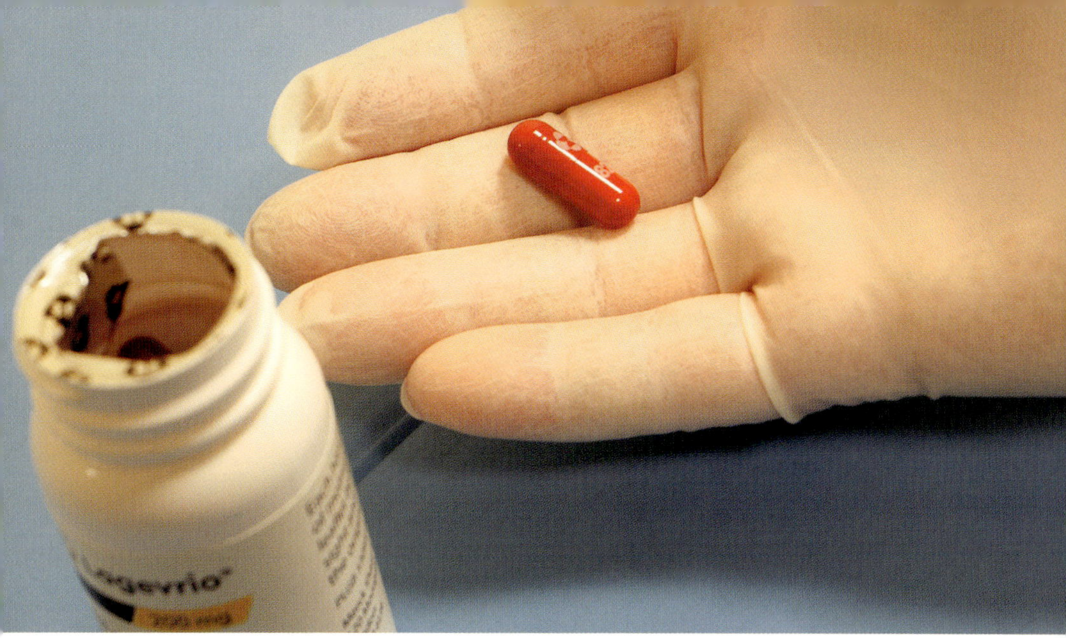

Molnupiravir was sold under the trademark name Lagevrio.

and deaths. Molnupiravir, an oral antiviral medication for COVID-19 developed by Merck, was also granted an EUA by the FDA in December 2021. These prescription medications can be picked up at a local drug store and taken at home without a hospital admission.

COVID-19 was still a deadly disease. But improvements in care and treatments showed promise. According to a study published in March 2021, mortality rates of COVID-19 patients in US hospitals dropped from 22.1 percent in March 2020 to 6.5 percent in August of that year.[12] As the pandemic continued, doctors learned more about how COVID-19 affects the body and the best strategies to treat it. At the same time, the world waited for an effective vaccine against COVID-19.

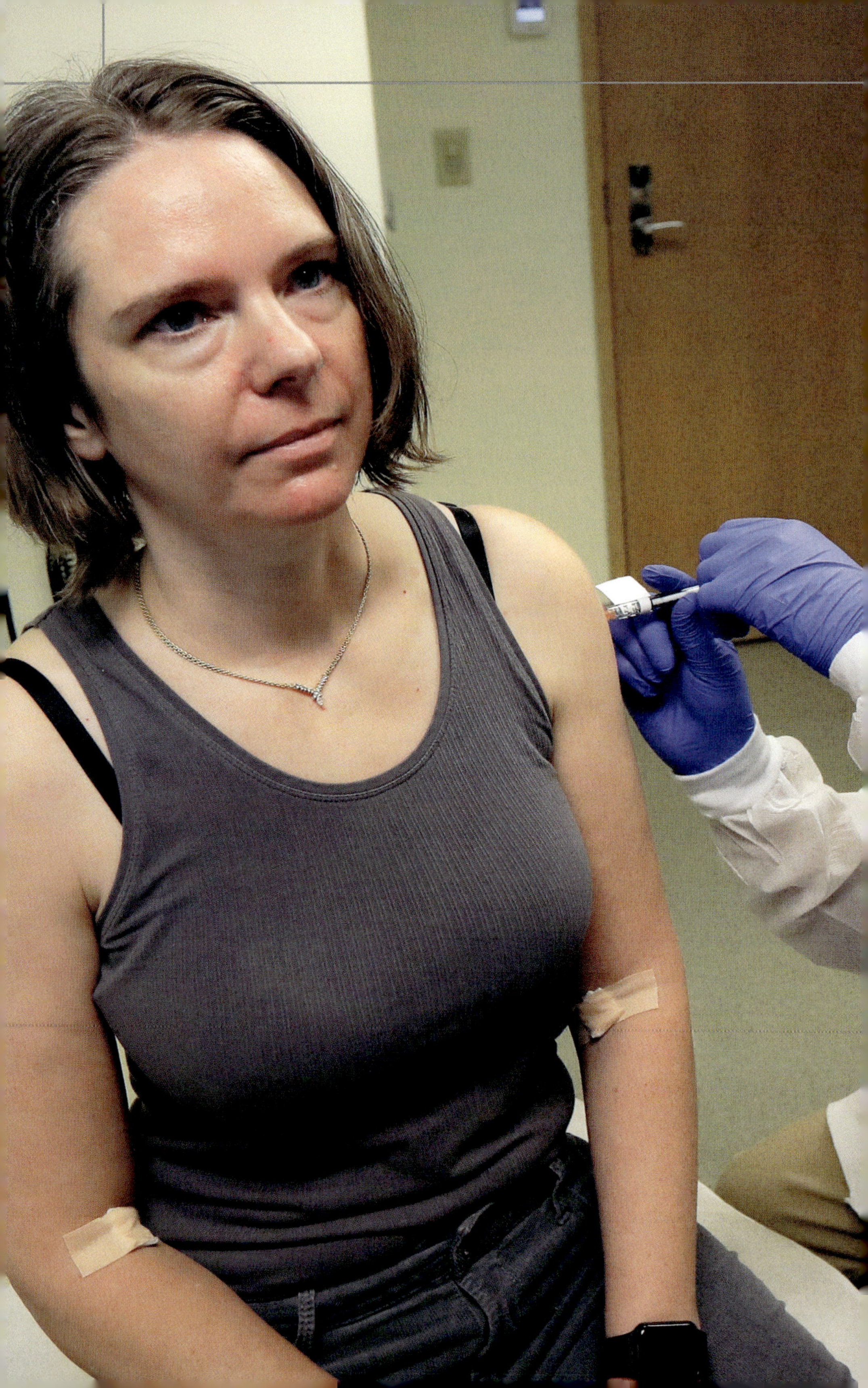

CHAPTER FOUR

VACCINE RESEARCH

Months before Sandra Lindsay made history as the first person in the United States to receive a SARS-CoV-2 vaccine under the FDA's EUA, another woman, Jennifer Haller, was rolling up her sleeve in Seattle, Washington, to get an experimental vaccine against the virus. Only 75 days after news of the mysterious pneumonia cases in Wuhan had surfaced, 43-year-old Haller volunteered to be one of the world's first COVID-19 vaccine trial subjects because she thought it was the right thing to do. On March 16, 2020, Haller became the first person to receive a COVID-19 vaccine in a clinical trial. She said at the time, "We all feel so helpless. This is an amazing opportunity for me to do something."[1]

To some people, it seemed like the experimental vaccine Haller received was rushed. However, the research needed to create it had begun years earlier. Previously, scientists at various institutions, including

Jennifer Haller receives the first SARS-CoV-2 vaccine in a US clinical trial.

BioNTech and Massachusetts-based Moderna, worked independently to use a molecule called messenger ribonucleic acid (mRNA) to teach the body's immune system how to fight disease.

Inside the nucleus of every cell in the human body, a deoxyribonucleic acid (DNA) molecule stores genetic instructions that cells use to make proteins. Proteins are the body's workers. They carry out almost every function in the human body. Also inside the cell, structures called ribosomes make the proteins the body needs. Because DNA does not leave the cell's nucleus, mRNA carries the genetic instructions from the DNA to the ribosomes so that the cell can make the proteins the body needs. Scientists believed mRNA could also teach the body to make antibody proteins to fight infection.

Traditional vaccines often use a weakened or inactivated virus or a piece of the virus's protein coat to teach the immune system what the virus looks like and how to fight it. However, growing large amounts of virus and preparing it for use in vaccines is complicated and takes a lot of time. Scientists hoped mRNA could be used as a simpler way to make vaccines because it is relatively easy to make.

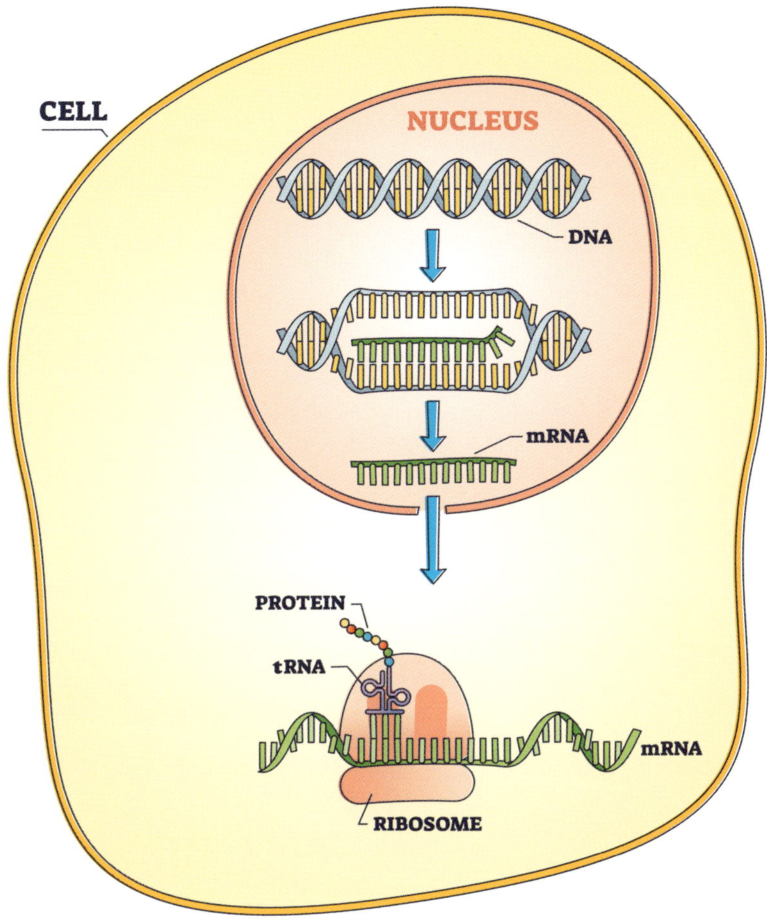

Within a cell's nucleus, mRNA is made as an inexact copy of a segment of DNA. From there, it can move to a ribosome, where transfer RNA (tRNA) helps decode the mRNA's information to create certain proteins.

Scientists researched ways to use mRNA in vaccines. They had also studied coronaviruses and other viruses to learn how they spread and attack the body. They gathered data about each type of virus's structure, life cycle, and genome. By 2017, scientists had discovered how to mimic a protein on the surface of a coronavirus. With this knowledge, they were one step closer to creating an mRNA vaccine. Researchers did not know it at the time, but the years of studying mRNA and coronaviruses had prepared them for what would be needed to create a vaccine for SARS-CoV-2.

AWARD-WINNING BREAKTHROUGH

In September 2021, two scientists responsible for the technology used in both the Pfizer-BioNTech and Moderna COVID-19 vaccines won the prestigious Lasker Award, often known as America's Nobel Prize. Scientists Drew Weissman and Katalin Karikó from the University of Pennsylvania shared the 2021 Lasker Clinical Medical Research Award for their work to develop mRNA technology. Their groundbreaking 2005 study on mRNA proved that it was possible to alter mRNA and deliver it into the body to create a protective immune response. The technology allows labs to make vaccines much more quickly and enabled Pfizer-BioNTech and Moderna to develop effective COVID-19 vaccines in months instead of years.

PRELIMINARY WORK BEGINS

When word of a new coronavirus broke in January 2020, Barney Graham, deputy director of the Vaccine Research Center at the

NIH, gathered a team of scientists who had years of experience working with vaccines, mRNA, and coronaviruses. The team worked together to use what it already knew about coronaviruses and mRNA to tailor a vaccine specifically to the new coronavirus. Years of research on coronavirus vaccines in mice helped to speed the team's work. At the same time other scientists around the world, including those with Pfizer and BioNTech, were also racing to develop COVID-19 vaccines.

ANIMAL MODELS

Animal research is an essential part of developing safe and effective vaccines. Before a promising vaccine candidate can be tested in humans, the FDA requires that it first be tested for safety and effectiveness in animals. Scientists determine if the vaccine candidate safely produces an effective immune response in these animal studies. Often, animal studies start with small animals and later involve larger animals. Mice are frequently used in animal studies because they reproduce quickly.

Graham's team planned an mRNA vaccine that would trigger the body to produce a protein identical to the distinctive spike protein on the surface of the SARS-CoV-2 virus. The virus's spikes protrude from its surface and help it latch on to a healthy cell and invade it. That protein produced in response to the mRNA vaccine would trigger the body's immune system to start making the correct antibodies it needed to fight SARS-CoV-2. Graham's team consulted with Moderna scientists. Moderna used the genetic code Graham's team provided to produce the vaccine. Together, they planned the first clinical trial of the vaccine.

Before the vaccine could be tested in humans, scientists needed to prove its effectiveness in mice. In February, Moderna shipped its first doses of COVID-19 vaccines to the NIH to use in the mice studies. Results later that month confirmed that the vaccinated mice were producing antibodies to fight the virus.

TESTING VACCINES IN HUMANS

Planning the first human trials was the next step. Human clinical trials occur in several phases in which the safety, effectiveness, and dosage of a vaccine or medicine are analyzed. Typically, in a phase 1 trial, a small number of people are studied to see if a vaccine is safe and triggers an immune response in the body. In a phase 2 trial, investigators look at a larger number of people with similar characteristics, such as age and health, as the people for whom the vaccine is intended. In a phase 3

During clinical trials, researchers tested participants' blood to check for antibodies to help determine if the vaccine would work.

trial, thousands of people receive the vaccine and are studied to see how well it works and ensure it is safe.

The first Moderna trial involved three groups of 15 adults each.[2] The participants received two shots 28 days apart. In this first trial, scientists wanted to determine if the vaccine produced the proper antibodies and start determining the correct dosage. They also wanted to see if it caused any side effects. If any serious side effects

SAFETY MONITORING

Even after a vaccine has been granted an EUA or been fully approved, scientists continue to collect safety data. For two more years, they follow study participants who received the vaccine. This continued monitoring gives scientists and the public more reassurance that the vaccine is safe and effective in real-world use.

appeared, the trial would be immediately stopped. On March 16, Jennifer Haller got her first shot.

The first results from the phase 1 clinical trial came in by early May 2020, showing that the vaccine produced COVID-19 antibodies in all 45 participants. When researchers took the antibodies and tested them on infected cells in the laboratory, the antibodies stopped the virus from replicating. Days later, Moderna announced plans for a phase 2 clinical trial with 600 volunteers, which was used to determine the correct vaccine dose.[3] Moderna also started planning for a larger phase 3 clinical trial to begin in July.

On July 27, Moderna's phase 3 clinical trial began. The trial was conducted at nearly 100 research sites and enrolled about 30,000 volunteers.[4] Investigators used the trial to further evaluate the vaccine's safety and effectiveness at preventing COVID-19 after two doses. In this type of trial, called a double-blind trial, computers assigned a code number and treatment group to each volunteer. Based on their treatment group, volunteers received either a vaccine shot or a placebo shot. Neither the volunteers nor the investigators knew who got which shot until after the study was completed. At this time, the Moderna trial was one of 25 ongoing clinical COVID-19 vaccine trials worldwide.[5]

A WORLDWIDE EFFORT

Typically, vaccine clinical trials take years to complete. However, several factors allowed scientists to accelerate the development of COVID-19 vaccines. Everyone worldwide was affected by the pandemic, and this common threat prompted researchers, companies, and governments to share information and prioritize research and clinical trials. Advances in genomic sequencing allowed researchers to decode the gene sequence of SARS-CoV-2 weeks after its discovery.

Funding from governments and private sector companies also helped speed the COVID-19 vaccine work. In the United States, the Trump administration launched a federal vaccine initiative called Operation Warp Speed (OWS), in which multiple government agencies, including

Dr. Francis Collins, then director of the NIH, helped guide OWS.

the NIH and the CDC, and private companies teamed up to develop and distribute COVID-19 vaccines. The chances of a vaccine being available quickly increased because OWS funded multiple vaccine research projects simultaneously.

> **"[The development of the COVID-19 vaccines] shows how fast vaccine development can proceed when there is a true global emergency and sufficient resources."[6]**
>
> *—Dan Barouch, director of the Center for Virology and Vaccine Research at Harvard Medical School*

Sometimes vaccine development can be slow because it is challenging to recruit the large numbers of volunteers needed to complete clinical trials. However, for the COVID-19 vaccines, thousands of people quickly volunteered for the trials, allowing the trials to proceed faster than expected. A large number of testing sites to enroll volunteers and collect data also helped speed up the process.

OPERATION WARP SPEED

To quickly develop and distribute a COVID-19 vaccine, the US federal government under President Trump announced the launch of OWS in May 2020. The program provided $10 billion in funding to support companies in vaccine development and the manufacturing and distribution of 300 million doses of an approved COVID-19 vaccine, with the first doses to be ready by January 2021.[8] Many people viewed OWS as a success when two vaccines—from Pfizer and Moderna—were developed and authorized for emergency use in less than a year.

By early November 2020, the news had come in that the phase 3 mRNA vaccine trials were successful. The mRNA vaccines from both Pfizer and Moderna were highly effective at preventing COVID-19. Albert Bourla, Pfizer chair and CEO, said, "We could not have come this far without the tremendous commitment of everyone involved."[7]

CHAPTER FIVE

HOW DO THE VACCINES WORK?

Every day, microorganisms try to invade the human body. Infectious agents such as bacteria, viruses, fungi, and parasites typically enter the body through food, water, or air and cause infection and sickness. The body's immune system uses its defensive methods to try and prevent sickness. The immune system attacks these pathogens that cause disease. Vaccines also help the immune system protect the body against disease.

The immune system is made up of a network of cells, tissues, and organs. One of the main components is white blood cells. White blood cells seek out and destroy disease-causing pathogens. The body produces and stores white blood cells in several places, including the bone marrow, thymus, and spleen.

There are vaccines to help protect people from many kinds of illnesses.

TYPES OF IMMUNITY

The human body has three types of immunity: innate, adaptive, and passive. Humans are born with innate immunity, a general protection. Innate immunity is the body's first line of defense against harmful invaders such as viruses, bacteria, and more. Innate immunity provides a general response to any invader detected in the body and attempts to stop the invader's spread in the body. In contrast, adaptive immunity is specific to certain diseases and pathogens. Adaptive immunity develops throughout a person's lifetime as the body is exposed to different diseases and produces antibodies against them. Adaptive immunity also occurs when a person receives a vaccine. Adaptive immunity takes longer to respond than innate immunity, but it provides a targeted response to a specific pathogen. Passive immunity occurs when short-term immunity is passed from one person to another, as when a baby gets antibodies through the mother's milk. This provides temporary immunity to the baby.

Lymphocytes are a type of white blood cell that remembers pathogens and helps fight them. There are two types of lymphocytes. B lymphocytes travel around the body and search for targets. When they find a pathogen, they produce specialized proteins that lock on to and tag the pathogen. These proteins are called antibodies. Antibodies signal other white blood cells to attack the pathogen. Each antibody attaches to a specific pathogen and either neutralizes it or tags it so that other immune cells, including T lymphocytes, will neutralize it.

The T lymphocytes rush to the pathogen and attack it. Other white blood cells join in to destroy the pathogen.

Once the immune system produces antibodies, they stay in the body, although they may diminish over time. If the immune system detects the same pathogen again, the antibodies are ready to fight. This type of learned immunity is called adaptive immunity.

Vaccines use the body's immune system to fight pathogens. When people are vaccinated for a disease, they typically receive a small amount of the pathogen, which may be inactivated or weakened. The dose is not large enough to make the person sick, but it triggers the body's immune system to produce antibodies. Sometimes, the vaccine will cause minor symptoms such as fever and chills. These symptoms are normal and part of the body's natural process of fighting infection. Once the vaccine's fake infection goes away, the antibodies produced remain in the body.

IMMUNITY AND AGE

As people age, their immune systems do not function as well as they once did. For this reason, the elderly are often more susceptible to disease and take longer to heal than younger people. This is also why the elderly are more vulnerable to severe disease when infected by SARS-CoV-2.

NATURALLY ACQUIRED IMMUNITY

When a person becomes infected with the SARS-CoV-2 virus and develops COVID-19, the immune system naturally produces antibodies to fight the infection. Once the person recovers, the body has naturally acquired immunity against the virus for some time. In 2022, scientists believed that natural immunity against SARS-CoV-2 lasted at least 90 days after infection.[1] However, they needed more data to confirm this.

The immune system can use these antibodies to attack the real pathogen if it invades the body in the future.

mRNA VACCINES

In the United States, three main types of COVID-19 vaccines were developed. Each type of vaccine triggers the body's immune system to recognize the SARS-CoV-2 virus and protect the person from COVID-19. An mRNA vaccine uses the mRNA's function of delivering protein-building instructions to teach the body how to make antibodies that will fight the SARS-CoV-2 virus. When injected into a person, an mRNA COVID-19 vaccine delivers the coronavirus's spike protein genetic material to cells. The cells use this information to produce their own version of the spike protein. After the cells make copies of the spike protein, the mRNA vaccine then naturally degrades within the cells so the cells no longer produce the spike protein.

The body's immune system views the harmless spike protein as an invader, and it produces antibodies to defend the body against attack. When a person becomes infected with the SARS-CoV-2 virus in the future, the body remembers the spike proteins and deploys the antibodies to neutralize the virus. The Pfizer-BioNTech and Moderna COVID-19 vaccines are mRNA vaccines.

VIRAL VECTOR VACCINES

> "It may be hard to imagine life without fear of the virus. But because we know the COVID-19 vaccines will be safe and effective, we know we're on the path to get there."[2]
>
> *—Shana Miles, a doctor with a PhD in emerging infectious diseases, in December 2020*

A viral vector vaccine uses a harmless version of a different virus to carry and deliver genetic information about the target virus. Some vaccines for Ebola have used viral vector technology while other studies are investigating viral vector vaccines for diseases such as Zika, AIDS, and influenza. In a COVID-19 vaccine, the vector virus carries and delivers the gene that codes for the SARS-CoV-2 spike protein into the body. When it enters a cell, the

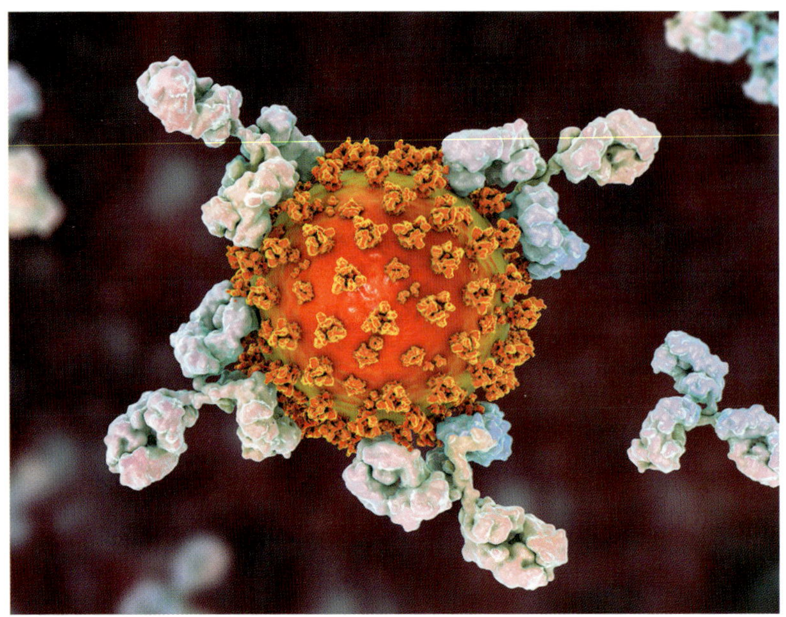

Antibodies, *white*, remember the spike proteins that jut from the surface of the virus and attach to the spikes.

vector virus delivers information that instructs the cells to produce the spike protein. As with the mRNA vaccine, the body's immune system recognizes this spike protein as an invader, produces antibodies, and fights the fake infection. In the future, the body will recognize the virus and remember how to fight it.

Viral vector vaccines cannot cause infection with either COVID-19 or the virus used as the vector. Johnson & Johnson's Janssen vaccine is a viral vector vaccine authorized for emergency use in the United States against SARS-CoV-2. AstraZeneca and the University of Oxford also developed a vector vaccine for COVID-19.

PROTEIN SUBUNIT VACCINE

A subunit vaccine uses harmless pieces of the SARS-CoV-2 virus instead of the entire virus. The vaccine delivers the virus pieces into the body, which recognizes them as foreign substances. The immune system gets to work producing antibodies and activating white blood cells to fight the invader. This immune response allows the body to fight future infections with the SARS-CoV-2 virus.

This type of vaccine technology has been used for years in vaccines for other diseases such as hepatitis B and pertussis (whooping cough). Novavax, an American biotechnology company, has developed a protein subunit vaccine for COVID-19. In January 2022, Novavax announced that it had filed a request for EUA for its COVID-19 vaccine.

MULTIPLE VACCINE DOSES

Some COVID-19 vaccines require a series of two shots. While developing the vaccines, scientists discovered that the mRNA vaccines produced a relatively weak immune response after a single shot. However, when patients received a second vaccine shot, the body's immune

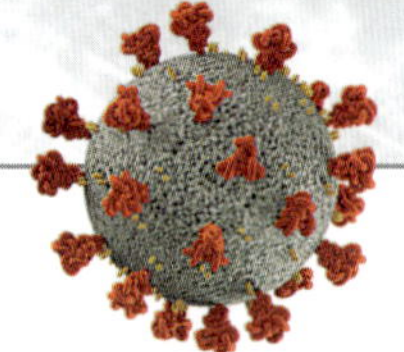

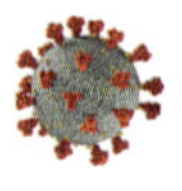

THE EFFECT OF VACCINATION ON COVID-19 DEATHS[3]

The COVID-19 vaccines proved extremely effective in preventing severe disease, hospitalization, and death in patients in the first half of 2021. In England, researchers tracked all COVID-19 deaths from January 2 to July 2, 2021. They found that COVID-19 vaccination provided strong protection to those infected with the virus. During this period, 76 percent of deaths occurred in people who had not been vaccinated at all. The risk of dying from COVID-19 dropped immediately after receiving even a single dose of a COVID-19 vaccine, and continued to decrease even further after completing the full two-dose vaccination program. Only 0.9 percent of the people who died had been more than 21 days past their second vaccine dose.

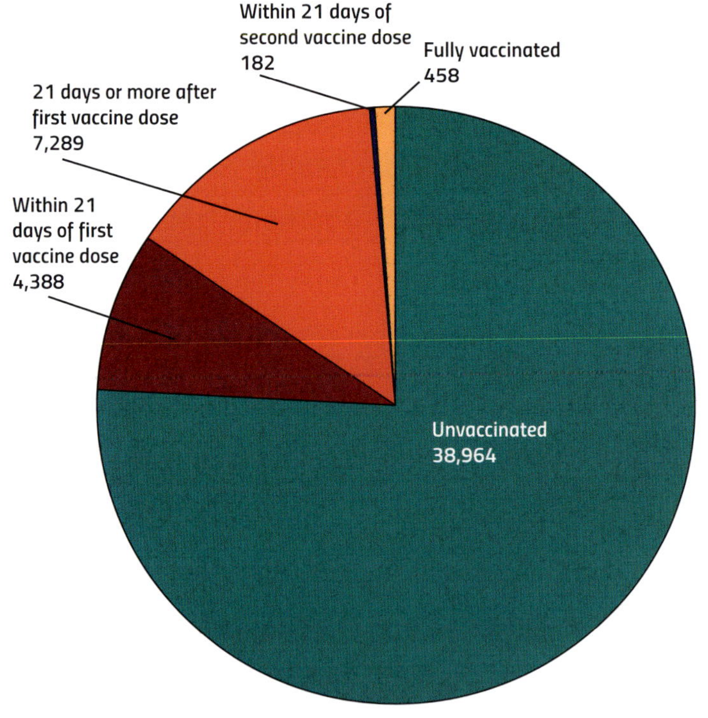

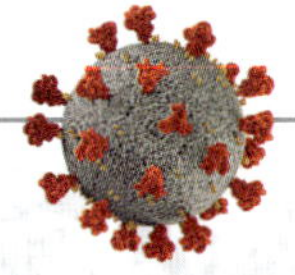

response was much stronger. The first dose gets the immune system to start producing antibodies to fight the virus. The second dose ramps up the antibody production and reinforces the immune system's ability to protect the body against disease.

PRIMARY DOSES

Some people's immune systems do not build enough immune protection against the virus that causes COVID-19 even after receiving all the standard doses in their primary vaccine series, which is the number of initial doses. For the COVID-19 vaccines, the Pfizer and Moderna vaccines are a two-dose primary series, while the Johnson & Johnson vaccine is a one-dose primary series. Often these people have compromised immune systems because of health conditions or medications that suppress the immune system. In these cases, doctors recommend that they receive an additional primary vaccine dose. This additional dose can help their immune systems mount a defense against the SARS-CoV-2 virus and prevent developing COVID-19.

Vaccines are an effective tool to fight infectious disease. They help the body's immune system build defenses against various pathogens, including the SARS-CoV-2 virus. The development of COVID-19 vaccines was an important step in reducing infections from SARS-CoV-2 and protecting people worldwide from severe disease and death.

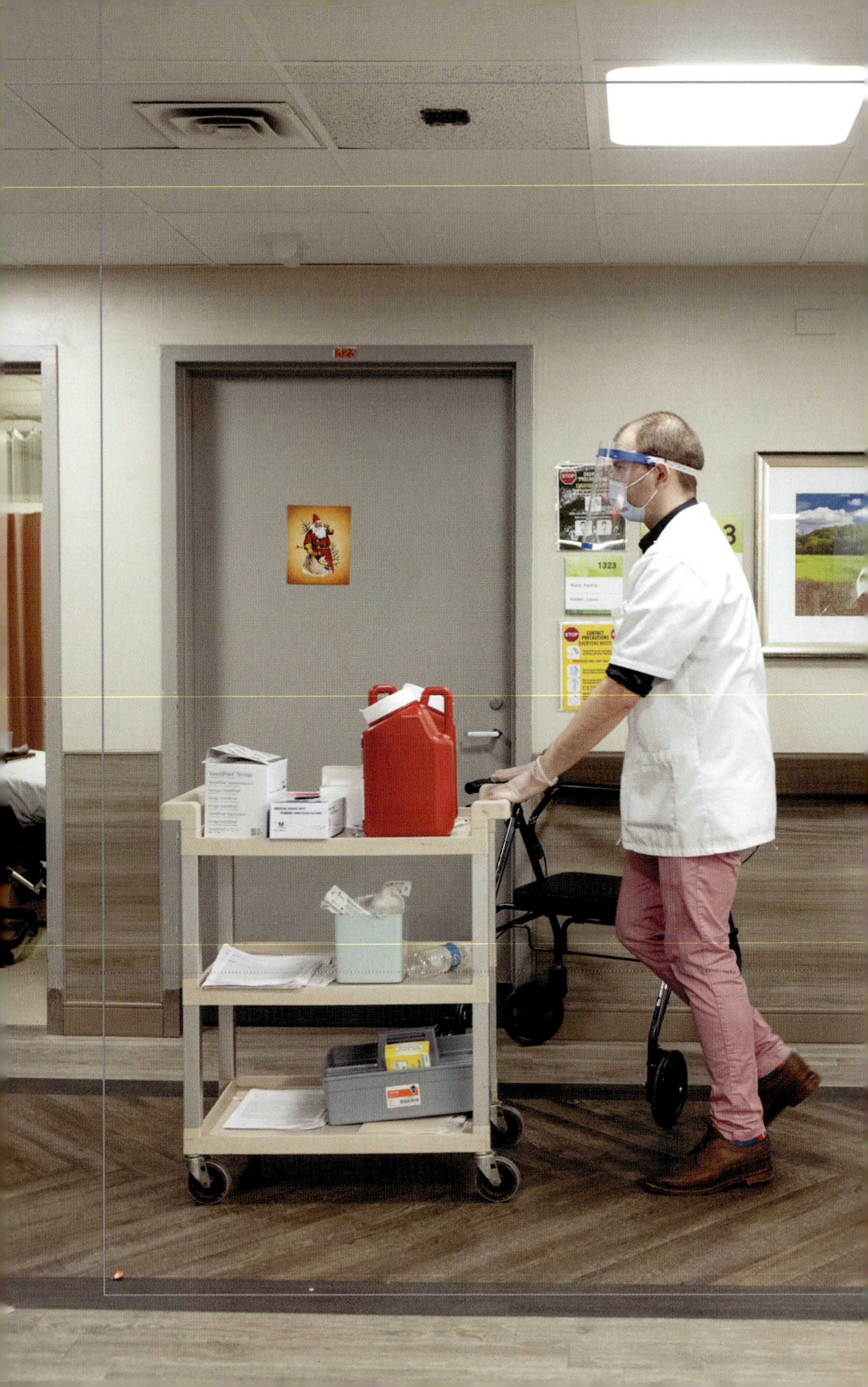
STOP
1323
STOP

CHAPTER SIX

VACCINATION CAMPAIGNS

After the first dose of a COVID-19 vaccine was given to Sandra Lindsay in New York, people around the United States began receiving it. News cameras across the country filmed the ritual of getting an injection. The vaccines had become a symbol of hope.

Within a few days of the FDA's emergency authorization of the Pfizer-BioNTech vaccine, trucks and cargo planes loaded with the first vaccine doses spread across the United States. Hospitals in all 50 states hurried to prepare vaccination sites. Because it would take time to make enough vaccine doses for everyone, the US government used phases for determining when to inoculate people. The specifics of each phase were decided state by state. In general, however, the people who faced the highest risk of contracting the

Residents and workers at places such as nursing homes were among the first to receive COVID-19 vaccines.

virus or developing severe disease were given priority to receive the vaccines. The first doses were often reserved for high-risk health-care workers and long-term care residents.

In the early days of the vaccine rollout, demand for the vaccines far exceeded the available supply. For many eligible people, finding an available vaccine appointment was frustrating. For Jane Heller, a 70-year-old Florida resident, it took almost four weeks. "I wanted to throw my computer out the window. It was so extremely frustrating," said Heller.[1] Sometimes, a person might book an appointment only to find it canceled later because the promised vaccine doses had not arrived.

EXPANDING VACCINE ELIGIBILITY

During February and March 2021, US vaccine eligibility slowly expanded to include other categories of essential workers and people deemed at higher risk of contracting COVID-19. By April, most Americans age 16 and older were eligible. At the time, the FDA had granted an EUA to three vaccines: the two-dose Pfizer and Moderna and the single-dose Johnson & Johnson vaccines. Communities and hospitals often set up large clinics in hospitals,

Early on, some vaccination sites needed extensive traffic control to manage the large number of people coming to get vaccinated.

stadiums, and community centers where hundreds of people could be vaccinated within hours.

At first, 40-year-old Marina B. was nervous about getting her vaccine, even though having type 2 diabetes put her at high risk of developing severe disease. "I felt scared of the side effects and the uncertainty over how long the shots would last," said Marina. Eventually, she decided that the risk of not getting vaccinated was too high. While waiting in line for her shot, Marina's anxiety soared. However, she quickly calmed after the shot. "There's no longer crippling anxiety when someone doesn't have their mask on. I'm still wearing my mask, but I'm no longer afraid of the outside world," she said.[2]

PUBLIC EDUCATION CAMPAIGNS

Since the vaccines first became available, the US government under President Joe Biden and local health agencies have launched numerous education and ad campaigns to encourage more people to get a COVID-19 vaccine. Some ads were aimed at increasing trust in the vaccines. Others promoted positive messages such as protecting the community and getting back to normal activities. For example, one set of ads featured scenes of friends hugging and children enjoying sleepovers.

In October 2021, the US Department of Health and Human Services (HHS) launched a different education campaign. The new ads highlighted the real-life consequences of not getting vaccinated and featured real people talking about their COVID-19 experiences. "We believe these first-person accounts of people who've experienced COVID firsthand can really underscore the danger that COVID-19 poses," said an HHS official.[3]

In one ad, Amanda from Richwood, Ohio, told of her experience surviving COVID-19. "I got COVID. I was intubated and in a coma for 11 days. . . . I did not get the COVID vaccine. I was concerned about some of the side effects. However, if I had it to do over, I would definitely go get the COVID vaccine. I know that I was very close to death. The fact that I almost did not come home to my husband and to my children is terrifying," she said in the ad.[4]

SHOTS AT THE SHOP

Several vaccine campaigns have specifically targeted people of color to ease fears about vaccination and provide accurate information about vaccination. One campaign that launched in 2021 was created through a partnership between the Black Coalition against COVID and the White House. Together, they launched a campaign called Shots at the Shop in hopes of reaching more people in the Black community and persuading them to get vaccinated. Because hair salons and barbershops are often gathering spots and community hubs, the campaign recruited salons and shops to host vaccine clinics and distribute information about the COVID-19 vaccines. Mike Brown, owner of the Shop Spa in Hyattsville, Maryland, hosted a vaccine clinic at his barbershop in May 2021. At the clinic, more than 30 people got vaccinated, many of whom were hesitant before getting their shot.[5]

MAKING PROGRESS ON VACCINATION

In early May 2021, the federal government launched several initiatives to make

Vaccine ads were placed in highly trafficked areas such as subway stations, where many people would see them.

vaccinations more accessible to Americans. It announced plans to offer more walk-in appointments, support pop-up clinics, expand smaller community vaccination sites and mobile clinics, send more vaccines to rural clinics, and provide additional funding to communities for outreach to persuade more people to get vaccinated.

According to the CDC, by early August 2021, 70 percent of eligible Americans were at least partially vaccinated.[6] About 50 percent of the country's total population was fully vaccinated.[7] The 70 percent milestone was seen by many as an important step toward the country reaching herd immunity, which is when enough people in a community carry antibodies against a disease that the virus begins to run out of people to infect.[8]

However, some infectious disease experts urged caution. Pockets of the country with low vaccination rates remained. Natasha Bhuyan, a family physician with One Medical in Phoenix, Arizona, said, "Even if America reaches 70 percent or 75 percent, if we continue to have ZIP codes and neighborhoods at 40 or 50 percent, they will continue to be at risk of having outbreaks and being hot spots. Even if we hit the 70 percent milestone, we can celebrate but we should celebrate it with caution."[9]

VACCINE INCENTIVES

To encourage people to get their COVID-19 vaccine, states and cities offered incentives. Some states offered free tickets to attractions. In Illinois, the Six Flags Great America amusement park offered 50,000 free tickets to newly vaccinated Illinois residents, while in New Jersey, vaccinated residents could receive a free state park pass. Other states offered financial incentives. In West Virginia, every vaccinated resident could receive a $100 savings bond. And some states went big with their incentives. In Colorado, the Colorado Comeback Cash vaccine drive awarded five people $1 million each for getting vaccinated.[10]

REAL-WORLD RESULTS

With millions of people worldwide getting vaccinated, scientists had plenty of data to analyze the real-world effectiveness of the COVID-19 vaccines. In clinical trials, scientists report a vaccine's efficacy, which is how well it prevents disease under ideal and controlled conditions. Some COVID-19 vaccines reported greater than 90 percent efficacy in preventing symptomatic disease in clinical trials.[11]

In contrast, effectiveness measures how well a vaccine performs in the real world, where conditions may not always be perfect. In the real world, the vaccine faces any new virus variants that emerge. It is used in people who may have been excluded from clinical trials, such as those who are frail and sick.

In late March 2021, the CDC announced the results of a study of the effectiveness of the Pfizer and Moderna

MISINFORMATION

As vaccine campaigns appeared nationwide, vaccine misinformation also spread through communities. Misinformation is content that is inaccurate, false, or misleading. Misinformation about COVID-19 vaccines appeared on all major social media platforms, online forums, and other places online and in the real world. Examples of vaccine misinformation included conspiracy theories, misleading statistics, and headlines that misrepresented the underlying facts and data. Some of the misinformation about the COVID-19 vaccines involved false claims that the vaccines caused infertility, vaccine development was rushed and unsafe, and the vaccines changed a person's DNA.

vaccines in real-world conditions. The study followed about 4,000 health-care professionals, police officers, firefighters, and other essential workers and found that the vaccines reduced the participants' risk of infection by 90 percent after two doses.[12] The findings highlighted how well the vaccines worked among a diverse group of adults whose jobs put them at high risk of being exposed to the virus. CDC director Rochelle Walensky explained that the study showed that the vaccines were working to protect people against infection and disease. She said, "These findings should offer hope to the millions of Americans receiving coronavirus vaccines each day and to those who will have the opportunity to roll up their sleeves and get vaccinated in the weeks ahead. The authorized vaccines are the key tool that will help bring an end to this devastating pandemic."[13]

"If you want to be part of the solution, get vaccinated."[14]

—Anthony Fauci, director of the National Institute of Allergy and Infectious Diseases, in December 2020

THE SCIENCE
ISN'T SETTLED,
IT'S CORRUPT

CHAPTER SEVEN

VACCINE HESITANCY AND MANDATES

Developing a safe vaccine to protect the world from COVID-19 was significant. However, it was only the first step toward ending the worldwide pandemic. A safe and effective vaccine must be accepted and used by the people for whom it is intended. As people worldwide celebrated the development of COVID-19 vaccines, many people rolled up their sleeves to get vaccinated. But others remained hesitant.

Vaccine hesitancy had the potential to derail efforts to bring the pandemic under control. In March 2021, a survey of American adults found that 62 percent had already gotten a COVID-19 vaccine or planned to do so as soon as possible. At the same time, 38 percent, or nearly four in ten Americans, were not ready to get vaccinated. Some 17 percent said they preferred

There were many reasons people were hesitant to get vaccinated, including a mistrust in government-funded science.

to wait and see, 7 percent planned to get vaccinated only if required, and 13 percent said they would not get vaccinated at all.[1]

The WHO defines vaccine hesitancy as a delay in accepting a vaccine or a refusal to get vaccinated despite the availability of an effective vaccine. In May 2021, a Gallup poll reported that 32 percent of adults worldwide, about 1.3 billion people, were unwilling to receive a free COVID-19 vaccine.[2] Governments faced the dilemma of how to persuade those hesitant or unwilling to get vaccinated to do so.

According to a September 2021 poll, there were several main reasons why some people were hesitant to get a COVID-19 vaccine. Some were concerned about possible side effects, while others wanted to wait and see if it was safe. Some did not trust the vaccines or

MAKING IT POLITICAL

In 2020, the country was increasingly becoming politically polarized. These deep divisions spilled over into the COVID-19 vaccination campaigns. While Democrats overwhelmingly supported vaccination efforts, many Republicans and Independents were less enthusiastic. In September 2021, a Gallup poll highlighted the differences. By mid-September, 92 percent of Democrats surveyed were vaccinated, while 68 percent of Independents and 56 percent of Republicans had received their COVID-19 vaccines.[3]

> "As the vaccination effort continues, it will be important to continue to adapt messages (and their messengers) to people who still remain hesitant."[5]
>
> —*Emily K. Brunson, associate professor of anthropology at Texas State University, on July 1, 2021*

the governments that promote them. Some believed that COVID-19 was not a serious disease and did not think they needed to be vaccinated.

Some people wanted to wait and see more data and evidence about the vaccines before getting vaccinated. They were worried that the COVID-19 vaccines were developed and tested too quickly. Others were firmly opposed to the vaccines. Angelique White, a 28-year-old hairstylist from Michigan, did not plan to get a vaccine. Even though several of her cousins had died from COVID-19, she remained firm in her decision. White and her twin sister fell violently ill after receiving a flu shot years ago. Since then, neither twin has gotten another vaccine. "I wear my mask, I sanitize my hands and do it like that. I think I'll be fine," White said.[4]

CONTINUED VIRUS SPREAD

High numbers of people unwilling to get vaccinated create a barrier to achieving herd immunity.

FULL FDA APPROVAL

On August 23, 2021, the FDA granted full approval of the Pfizer-BioNTech COVID-19 vaccine for people ages 16 and older. The Pfizer vaccine had been administered in the United States under an EUA since December 11, 2020. A vaccine must undergo a rigorous review for quality, safety, and effectiveness to receive FDA approval. "The public can be very confident that this vaccine meets the high standards for safety, effectiveness, and manufacturing quality the FDA requires of an approved product," said acting FDA commissioner Janet Woodcock. "While millions of people have already safely received COVID-19 vaccines, we recognize that for some, the FDA approval of a vaccine may now instill additional confidence to get vaccinated."[8] On January 31, 2022, the FDA also granted full approval of the Moderna COVID-19 vaccine for people ages 18 and older.

Herd immunity protects the vulnerable members of a community who cannot get vaccinated. "Even though a person may not have immunity for whatever reason—maybe they don't have a strong immune system, they're unable to get the vaccine or children are the obvious example right now—what we do is we surround them. We insulate them from the virus by having everybody around them have immunity," said Thompson W. Liddell, an infectious disease specialist.[6] Some experts have estimated that 90 percent of the total population would need to be fully vaccinated for the United States to reach herd immunity protection against SARS-CoV-2.[7]

Large pockets of unvaccinated people allow the virus to continue spreading in communities. They also give the virus the chance to mutate into deadlier and more transmissible variants. When a virus enters the body, it replicates and spreads. Sometimes, when the virus copies itself, there are some changes in its genetic code. These changes are called mutations. Mutations can change how the virus works, making it better at spreading or more likely to cause severe illness. Scientists worried that unvaccinated people not only would put themselves at greater risk of disease but also would increase the risk of a variant emerging that could evade vaccines. "The more people [the virus] has that are vulnerable or susceptible to infection, the more likely it will mutate," said Dr. Michael Saag, a professor of medicine and infectious diseases at the University of Alabama at Birmingham.[9]

VACCINE MANDATES

Some cities, businesses, schools, and governments decided to mandate vaccination to get more people vaccinated. A vaccine mandate is a requirement that states a person must be vaccinated to work, travel, attend a concert, or do other things. A government, business, or other organization cannot force a person to get vaccinated. However, if a person chooses not to get a vaccine, these entities can legally prevent an unvaccinated person from entering a building, using services, attending class, or holding a job.

In July 2021, New York City mayor Bill de Blasio announced a vaccine mandate for all health-care workers in the city. Workers needed to be fully vaccinated or submit to weekly COVID-19 testing. Workers who refused both options could be suspended without pay. There would be limited exceptions for medical or religious reasons.

Other mandates soon followed. California became the first state to mandate vaccination for all health-care

ARE MANDATES EFFECTIVE?

Although vaccine mandates have sparked protests and lawsuits, data supports their effectiveness. Some businesses have reported that employee vaccination rates have jumped significantly after a workplace mandate went into effect. For example, when Tyson Foods announced its vaccine mandate on August 3, 2021, less than half of its nearly 140,000 employees were vaccinated. By the end of October, 96 percent of company staff were vaccinated.[10] Tyson Foods president and CEO Donnie King noted that employees getting vaccinated made a real difference in the health and safety of Tyson's workers. With more vaccinations, the company had seen a significant decline in active COVID-19 cases.

and state workers in August 2021. After the FDA's full approval of the Pfizer vaccine on August 23, several corporations including Disney, General Electric, and Goldman Sachs issued vaccine mandates for employees. In late August, the Pentagon ordered all active-duty service members to be vaccinated against COVID-19. In September, Los Angeles County Unified School District mandated that all children age 12 and older be vaccinated. Also in September, President Biden announced a plan to mandate that all private companies with more than 100 employees must require COVID-19 vaccinations or have workers undergo weekly testing.

New York City announced a mandate for all on-site employees for private businesses in December 2021. Some people applauded the requirement to get

PAST MANDATES

Vaccine mandates have a long history in the United States. In the 1800s, many cities and states began requiring children to be immunized against smallpox, a contagious disease that killed three out of every ten people infected.[11] In 1905, the US Supreme Court upheld in *Jacobson v. Massachusetts* a decision that the state could impose mandatory vaccinations on its citizens to protect public health and safety. Since then, most US states have required several vaccinations for children to attend school. Some states have vaccine mandates for specific categories of adults. For example, in New York, all workers in hospitals, nursing homes, and other health-care facilities must be immunized against measles and rubella.

In some schools, the COVID-19 vaccines were added to the list of mandatory vaccines for students.

vaccinated. However, other New Yorkers opposed the mandate. Some, such as Khaleem Majid, had mixed feelings. Majid, who was fully vaccinated, worked as a barber at a shop in the Bronx. "I hate the point when they're like, OK, you have to get vaccinated or you are getting fired. But also, hey, you're going to bring a virus and infect everybody in the job," he said.[12]

Some states, businesses, and other groups filed lawsuits to block federal COVID-19 vaccine mandates. Proponents of the vaccine mandates argued that they were necessary to stop the spread of COVID-19. Opponents argued that federal mandates were not authorized by the US Congress and infringed on states' rights to regulate public health matters. In late 2021, judges put several mandates on hold while the courts considered the cases.

In January 2022, the US Supreme Court issued two rulings on federal vaccine mandates. In one ruling, the court struck down the Biden administration's federal vaccine mandate for private employers with more than 100 employees. At the same time, the court upheld a federal vaccine mandate that required all facilities receiving federal Medicare and Medicaid funds to ensure all health-care staff were vaccinated, with certain exemptions. Numerous challenges to state, local, and employer vaccine mandates were also filed to be evaluated by the courts on a case-by-case basis.

OPPOSING VACCINATIONS

A small number of people around the world oppose the use of all vaccinations. These people, known as anti-vaxxers, oppose vaccination for all diseases. Generally, anti-vaxxers believe that vaccines are unsafe and their use violates human rights. Often, anti-vaxxers do not believe scientific evidence that supports the use and effectiveness of vaccinations. In the United States, the anti-vaccination movement has a long history, beginning in the 1700s when religious leaders compared vaccines to the devil's work. Today, although anti-vaxxers are a minority of the population, many are active on the internet and on social media platforms, where they have been accused of spreading misinformation about vaccines.

CHAPTER EIGHT

VARIANTS, DECLINING IMMUNITY, AND BOOSTER CONFUSION

Scientists constantly monitored the SARS-CoV-2 virus to identify any variants as they emerged. Variants have the potential to spread more quickly than previous versions of a virus, and some can cause more severe disease. As scientists studied the SARS-CoV-2 variants, they classified variants based on how easily they spread, how severe a disease they cause, how they respond to treatment, and how well vaccines protect against them. During the pandemic, multiple variants of the SARS-CoV-2 virus were identified and studied worldwide.

In January 2020, scientists identified one of the first mutations of the virus, which they named D614G. They believed the mutation stabilized the virus's spike protein

Variants of SARS-CoV-2 have been discovered in countries around the world. The Alpha variant was discovered in the United Kingdom.

to attach to human cells. The change made the virus more infectious. The mutated version of the virus quickly spread and replaced the original version.

THE DELTA VARIANT

As the virus spread, more mutations emerged, creating even more transmissible variants. A variant named Alpha emerged in November 2020 and was about 50 percent more infectious than the original virus.[1] In late 2020, scientists detected a worrisome variant of SARS-CoV-2 in India. The variant, known as the Delta variant, caused concern worldwide because of its ability to spread faster and cause more severe disease than earlier forms of the virus.

NAMING VARIANTS

Every virus variant has a scientific name that researchers use to convey important scientific information about the variant and its evolutionary history. However, these scientific names are often difficult for the general public to pronounce and remember. Therefore, the WHO assigned simple, easy-to-pronounce, and easy-to-remember names for variants of the SARS-CoV-2 virus. After consultation and review with experts worldwide, the WHO chose the letters of the Greek alphabet to name the SARS-CoV-2 variants. For example, the B.1.1.529 variant is commonly known as the Omicron variant, and the B.1.617.2 variant is known worldwide as the Delta variant.

By mid-2021, the Delta variant had spread worldwide. According to the CDC, by July it was the predominant variant in the United States and caused most new COVID-19 infections. Studies suggested that the Delta variant was highly contagious, more than twice as infectious as previous variants. “It is the most hypertransmissible, contagious version of the virus we’ve seen to date, for sure—it’s a super-spreader strain if there ever was one,” said Eric Topol, a professor of molecular medicine at the Scripps Research Institute.[2]

Some studies found that infection with the Delta variant may have caused more severe illness in unvaccinated people than previous variants. A study from Scotland published in the *Lancet* found that people infected with the Delta variant were 85 percent more likely to be hospitalized than those infected with previous variants.[3]

Scientists also discovered an increase in breakthrough infections, or infections occurring in people who are fully vaccinated. While the vaccines appeared to prevent severe illness, hospitalization, and death, some fully vaccinated people were being infected with the Delta variant. Fully vaccinated people could even spread the virus to others.

However, they did appear to spread the virus for a shorter period than unvaccinated infected people.

THE CASE FOR BOOSTERS

As the Delta variant infected people worldwide, scientists and medical experts debated the need for vaccine booster shots. A booster shot is an additional dose of a vaccine given to a person after the immunity provided by the original shot or shots has begun to lessen naturally over time. The booster shot aims to help people maintain high levels of immunity protection for a longer time.

Vaccine makers Pfizer, Moderna, and Johnson & Johnson urged the FDA and the

BOOSTER OR THIRD DOSE

Some immunocompromised patients have been encouraged to receive a third dose of a COVID-19 vaccine. Other adults have been authorized to receive a booster. Although it may sound the same, there can be a difference between the two. A COVID-19 additional dose or third shot is given to people with compromised immune systems. The additional dose improves their immune response and protection against the virus and is typically a full-strength dose. In comparison, a booster shot is given when a person has completed initial vaccination and the immune protection declines over time. A booster dose aims to restore immunity to previous high levels. In some cases, the booster dose is less than the original dose.

CDC to authorize booster shots for all Americans. At first, the CDC limited booster shots to high-risk groups. Then in November 2021, a study published in the journal *Science* reported that the effectiveness of the three approved vaccines declined over time. Pfizer's vaccine effectiveness decreased from 86 percent to 43 percent from February to October 2021. Moderna's vaccine effectiveness against symptomatic illness dropped from 89 percent to 58 percent, and Johnson & Johnson's vaccine fell from 86 percent to 13 percent over the same period.[4]

In November 2021, the FDA and CDC expanded booster authorization to all adults age 18 and older, and a month later expanded it again to include 16- and 17-year-olds. "Booster shots have demonstrated the ability to safely increase people's protection against infection and severe outcomes and are an important public health tool to strengthen our defenses against the virus as we enter the winter holidays," said CDC director Rochelle Walensky.[5] In January 2022, booster authorization expanded further to include children ages 12 and older.

Booster shots are not without controversy. Some people believe that the emphasis should be on getting unvaccinated people, both in the United States and worldwide, their first doses of a COVID-19 vaccine instead of administering booster shots. WHO director general Tedros Adhanom Ghebreyesus called the increasing use of boosters in some countries unfair when much of Africa remained unvaccinated. "To start boosters is really the worst we can do as a global community. It is unjust and also unfair because we will not stop the pandemic by ignoring a whole continent," he says.[6]

Many African countries, including Kenya, were not able to get enough vaccine doses to vaccinate a majority of their populations in 2021.

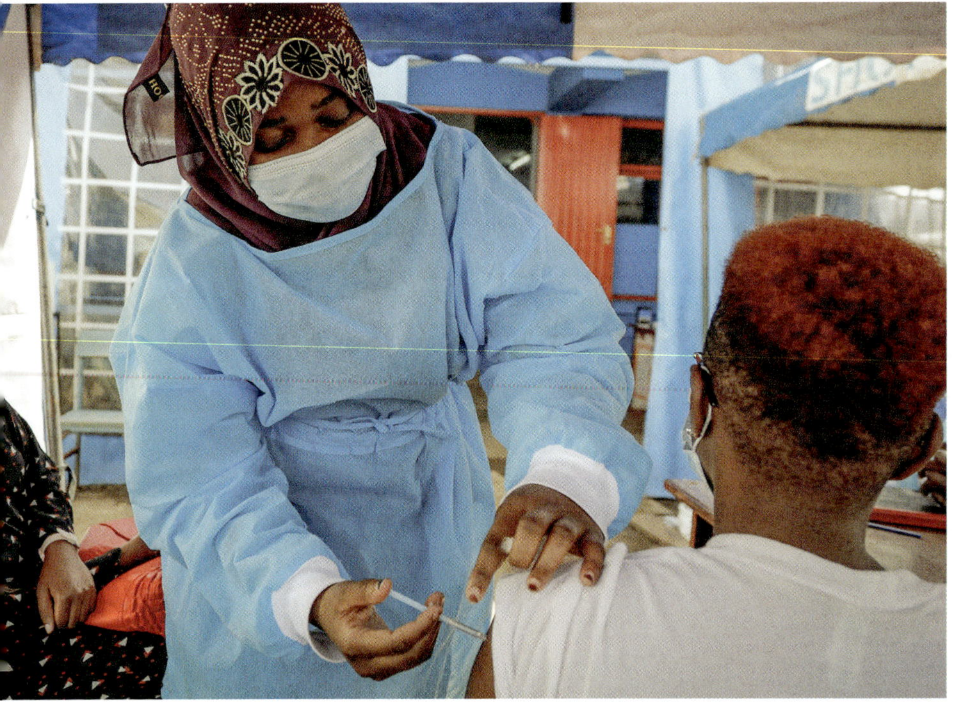

THE OMICRON VARIANT

> **"The more transmission, the more opportunity you have for variants to evolve."[7]**
>
> *—Steven Zeichner, an infectious disease expert and pediatrics professor at the University of Virginia School of Medicine in Charlottesville*

In November 2021, scientists detected a new variant of the SARS-CoV-2 virus in South Africa. The variant, named the Omicron variant, caused concern among public health officials and scientists because it contained an unusually high number of mutations. The many mutations make the Omicron variant more transmissible and less vulnerable to existing COVID-19 vaccines.

Within weeks, Omicron spread to numerous countries worldwide. By mid-December 2021, it was the dominant strain in the United States. Fears over the new variant triggered many nations to close their borders and restrict travel. Health officials urged all unvaccinated people to get vaccinated and eligible people to get their booster shots.

Meanwhile, scientists were working to better understand Omicron, how it spreads, whether it increases the risk of severe disease, and how effective vaccines

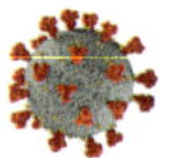

VACCINATION BY REGION[8]

Worldwide, more than 4.85 billion people had received at least one dose of a COVID-19 vaccine by February 10, 2022. That number was about 63 percent of the world's population. However, a closer look at who was vaccinated and who was not revealed inequities in vaccine access and distribution. This chart shows striking differences in the vaccination rates among the regions of the world. Less-wealthy regions relied on COVAX, a vaccine-sharing arrangement. COVAX originally promised to provide two billion doses by the end of 2021. However, it repeatedly cut its promised deliveries because of production problems, export bans, and vaccine hoarding in wealthy countries. As a result, a significant gap emerged between the regions of the world. In Africa, the region with the slowest vaccination rate, only 16 percent of its population was vaccinated with at least one dose by February 10.

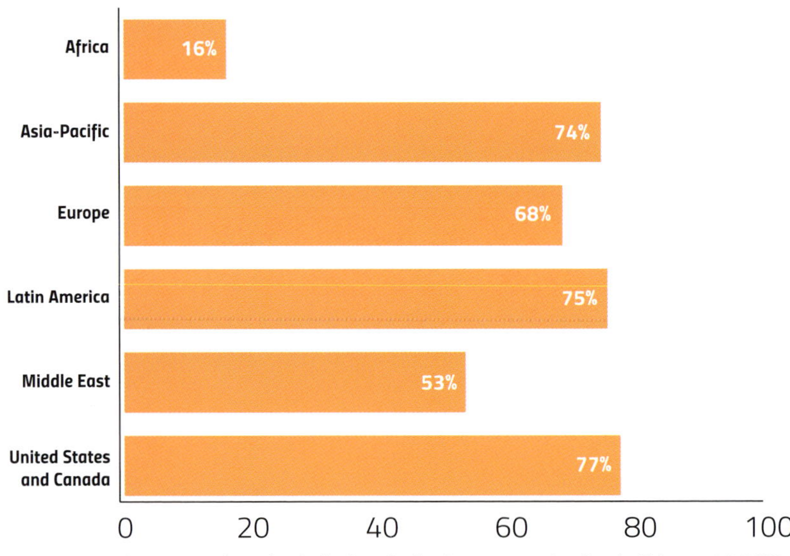

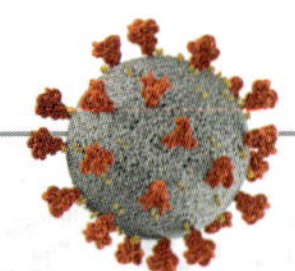

are against the variant. Early research showed that Omicron spread more quickly than Delta. Researchers looked at the households of 121 people infected with the Omicron variant in Britain. They found that Omicron was 3.2 times more likely to spread to another household member than the Delta variant.[9] Early research on vaccine effectiveness against Omicron suggested that people who had received a booster shot had higher levels of antibodies and could better fight an Omicron infection. As a result, efforts to get people vaccinated and distribute booster shots intensified. Scientists noted that while COVID-19 vaccines were less effective at preventing Omicron infection, the vaccines were able to prevent severe illness and death in most cases. And they would still help prevent mutations.

VACCINE FOR CHILDREN

On November 3, 2021, federal health officials officially approved the Pfizer COVID-19 vaccination for children ages five to 11. Previously, everyone age 12 and older was eligible for the vaccine. The pediatric dosage is one-third of the adult dose. However, many parents chose to wait before they got their young children vaccinated against COVID-19. In a December 2021 poll released by the Kaiser Family Foundation, about two-thirds of parents of elementary-aged children had either decided to wait to get their young children vaccinated or made up their minds that they would not be getting the vaccine at all.[10] For many parents, the lower risk of severe COVID-19 illness in young children and the potential for vaccine side effects reduced their motivation to vaccinate their kids.

Terminal 6
Gates 60-69
CLEAR
TSA Pre

CHAPTER NINE

THE FUTURE WITH COVID-19

What does the future hold for the virus that causes COVID-19? Viruses evolve over long periods. Most scientists doubt that the world will completely eradicate the SARS-CoV-2 virus. Although predicting what will happen in the future is extremely difficult, past scientific work on viruses may shed some light on the future with COVID-19.

The world's ability to slow SARS-CoV-2 infections may have a significant effect on the evolution of the virus. Every new infection creates another chance for the virus to mutate. "We have uncontrolled viral spread in much of the world. So the virus has a lot of opportunity to evolve," said Adam Lauring, a virologist and infectious disease physician at the University of Michigan.[1] While many mutations have little effect on a virus, others can

As long as people keep getting infected with SARS-CoV-2, the virus will have more chances to mutate.

ERADICATION

Most experts agree that complete eradication, or elimination, of SARS-CoV-2 is extremely unlikely. In history, only two diseases that affect humans or animals have ever been completely eradicated. Smallpox was a serious disease in humans that covered the body in painful blisters and could be deadly. Rinderpest was a viral disease that infected and killed cattle. For both diseases, successful global vaccination campaigns eventually stopped new infections. The last confirmed case of rinderpest occurred in 2001 in Kenya. The last confirmed case of smallpox was recorded in 1978 in the United Kingdom.

provide the virus with a survival advantage.

Mutations can change the SARS-CoV-2 virus in many ways; the world has already seen some possibilities with the variants that have emerged. In the future, scientists are concerned about mutations that could make the virus more transmissible, more harmful, or better at resisting the body's immune system.

WILL IT BECOME MORE TRANSMISSIBLE?

The SARS-CoV-2 virus has already mutated to become more transmissible. The Alpha variant was about 50 percent more infectious than the original virus. Later, the Delta variant emerged, which was about 50 percent more transmissible than Alpha.[2] The Omicron variant is even more transmissible than Delta.

The adaptation of the virus to become more transmissible was an expected change. Jesse Bloom is an expert in viral evolution at the Fred Hutchinson Cancer Research Center. In October 2021, he noted that it was still unclear how transmissible the SARS-CoV-2 virus could become. However, he and other scientists expected that there would be some biological limits on how infectious it would eventually be. For example, viruses such as measles and influenza are not constantly mutating to become more infectious every year. "Transmission requires one person to somehow exhale or cough or breathe out the virus, and it to land in someone else's airway and infect them," Dr. Bloom said. "There are just

PAN-VIRUS VACCINES

The SARS-CoV-2 pandemic has highlighted how highly transmissible and potentially deadly viruses can threaten human health. To respond to this threat, some scientists are calling for more investment and research into pan-virus vaccines and technologies that can respond to various virus types. One avenue of research focuses on broadly neutralizing antibodies. These antibodies can effectively respond to several strains of the same virus, not just one specific strain. They could be used to develop a vaccine that is effective against all mutations of a virus and eliminate the need for multiple vaccines for different variants.

Demand for COVID-19 testing rose in January 2022 because of the spread of Omicron.

limits to that process. It's never going to be the case that I'm sitting here in my office, and I'm giving it to someone on the other side of Seattle, right?"[3]

WILL IT LEARN TO EVADE THE IMMUNE SYSTEM?

Sometimes, mutations enable a virus to evade the immune system's defenses. The immune system produces antibodies that latch onto the virus's surface and prevent it from entering healthy cells. However, a mutation can change the virus's surface and shape. Antibodies can no longer attach to the virus and protect the body when this occurs. The immune system would eventually learn to make new antibodies to neutralize the variant, but this can take some time.

As more people produce antibodies from vaccination or natural infection, mutations that enable the virus to evade the immune system may become even more common. However, because there are many different types of antibodies, scientists believe it is unlikely that a variant with a few mutations will escape all of them. "The immune system has also evolved to have plenty of tricks up its sleeve to counteract the evolution of the virus. Knowing that there is this complex level of diversity in the immune system allows me to sleep better at night," said Marion Pepper, an immunologist at the University of Washington.[4]

WILL IT BECOME DEADLIER?

Mutations that make a virus more transmissible or more likely to evade the immune system give it a survival advantage. In contrast, mutations that make a virus more likely to cause severe disease give it no survival advantage. According to experts, this makes it more difficult to predict what will happen to the SARS-CoV-2 virus in the future.

Some experts suggest that mutations of the virus that cause more severe disease are less likely to spread because patients are often hospitalized. In contrast,

Researchers continue to study SARS-CoV-2, vaccines, and treatments.

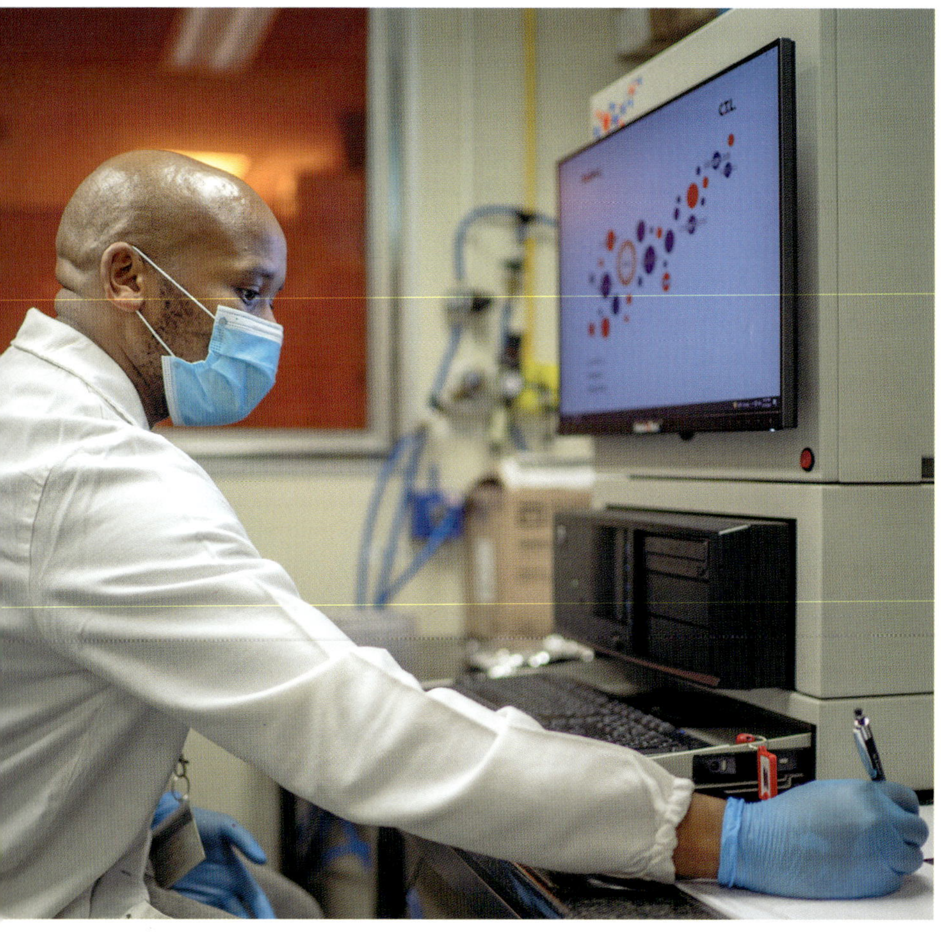

mutations that cause milder symptoms are more likely to spread as people go about their daily routine with a stuffy nose or headache. As a result, the virus may evolve to become milder.

One example of a virus becoming milder over time is the myxoma virus, which affects rabbits. In 1950, Australian scientists introduced the virus into a population of rabbits to reduce the number of an invasive European rabbit species. At first, the myxoma virus was very deadly and killed more than 99 percent of infected rabbits.[5] A few years later, milder variants of the virus emerged and became the most common variants. The rabbits' immune systems also evolved to better fight the virus.

Most scientists believe it is too early to predict if SARS-CoV-2 will become more or less deadly over time. "I could actually keep this game of imagining going on for a long time. On my good days, I'm optimistic that the disease severity will go down through time. Because clearly, people being isolated does affect transmission. On my bad days, I worry about it going the other direction," said Andrew Read, an evolutionary microbiologist at Penn State University, in October 2021.[6]

AN ENDEMIC FUTURE

As the virus evolves, the vaccines and treatments used to fight it will also evolve. Although the first vaccines were successful at fighting the virus, studies that allow scientists to refine doses and timing, or even tailor vaccines to new variants, may create even more effective tools against the virus. Additionally, if the number of infections declines and the spread slows because of vaccination and natural immunity, the virus will have fewer chances to mutate, and its evolution will slow. Occasional breakthrough infections could help the immune system recognize and fight new mutations.

Many scientists predict that the SARS-CoV-2 virus will eventually become an endemic disease, like the flu or the common cold. It will not

END OF THE PANDEMIC

In December 2021, several infectious disease experts predicted that the SARS-CoV-2 pandemic could end in 2022. When the worldwide spread of an infectious disease is brought under control, it moves from a pandemic to an epidemic, according to the WHO. An epidemic occurs when there is an outbreak of disease in a specific geographical area. If SARS-CoV-2 remained active at expected or normal levels in that area, the WHO would classify it as an endemic disease.

disappear completely. Instead, it will still circulate, but because most people will have gained immune protection, there will be less transmission and fewer cases of severe disease. In a *Nature* 2021 poll, almost 90 percent of experts researching COVID-19 said they believed it would become endemic and continue to circulate in areas of the world for years in the future.[7]

> "It's very unlikely that we're ever going to be able to get rid of Covid."[9]
>
> *—Timothy Brewer, a professor of epidemiology at the University of California, Los Angeles Fielding School of Public Health, in December 2021*

Annual COVID-19 vaccines, just like the yearly flu shot, may become a regular part of life. Time will tell what the future of COVID-19 will look like. "There may be multiple directions that the virus can go in, and the virus hasn't committed," said Andrew Rambaut, an evolutionary biologist at the University of Edinburgh.[8] The virus's future path hinges on the type of immunity people worldwide acquire—either through vaccination or infection—and how the virus adapts.

ESSENTIAL FACTS

KEY EVENTS

- On March 11, 2020, the World Health Organization declares COVID-19 a pandemic.
- On November 9, 2020, American biotechnology company Pfizer and its partner BioNTech, a German biotechnology company, announce they have successfully developed an effective vaccine against COVID-19.
- On December 14, 2020, Sandra Lindsay becomes the first American to receive a publicly available COVID-19 vaccine.
- In July 2021, New York City issues a vaccine mandate for all health-care workers in the city.
- By early August 2021, 70 percent of eligible Americans are at least partially vaccinated, and 50 percent are fully vaccinated, according to the CDC.
- On August 23, 2021, the FDA grants full approval to the Pfizer-BioNTech COVID-19 vaccine.
- In December 2021, the FDA grants an emergency use authorization for Pfizer's Paxlovid, an antiviral oral medication for the treatment of COVID-19.

KEY PEOPLE

- Jennifer Haller became the first person to receive an experimental COVID-19 vaccine as part of a clinical trial in March 2020.
- Barney Graham, deputy director of the Vaccine Research Center at the National Institutes of Health, gathered a team of scientists to develop a plan for the Moderna COVID-19 vaccine.

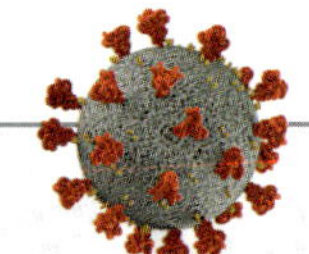

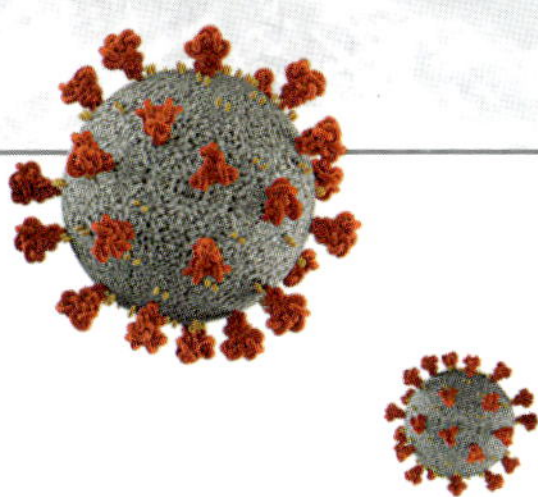

- Rochelle Walensky was the director of the Centers for Disease Control and Prevention, which had an essential role in the response to the COVID-19 pandemic.

KEY STATISTICS

- The SARS-CoV-2 virus killed nearly 6.2 million people worldwide by April 2022.
- A study released in March 2021 showed that the Pfizer and Moderna vaccines were more than 90 percent effective in preventing COVID-19 in real-world conditions.
- In seriously ill COVID-19 patients, blood oxygen levels can drop into the 60 to 70 percent range.
- In May 2021, a Gallup poll revealed that 32 percent of adults worldwide were not willing to receive a free COVID-19 vaccine.
- Preliminary studies suggested that Pfizer's antiviral COVID-19 medication decreases the risk of hospitalization or death by 89 percent if given within three days of symptoms emerging.

QUOTE

"These findings should offer hope to the millions of Americans receiving coronavirus vaccines each day and to those who will have the opportunity to roll up their sleeves and get vaccinated in the weeks ahead. The authorized vaccines are the key tool that will help bring an end to this devastating pandemic."

—Rochelle Walensky, CDC director

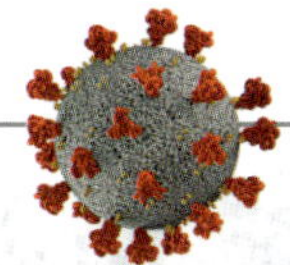

GLOSSARY

antibody

A protein that the immune system uses to fight infection.

asymptomatic

Not showing signs of an infection.

biotechnology

The use of living organisms or other biological systems in the manufacture of drugs or other products.

clinical trial

A type of research study that tests how well new medical approaches and treatments work in people.

convalescent

Recovering after an illness.

emergency use authorization

EUA; an authorization by the Food and Drug Administration that allows the use of a drug or treatment prior to full approval in order to make the product accessible during a state of emergency when no other viable alternative is available.

endemic

Something that is regularly found in a given environment.

genome

An organism's genetic material.

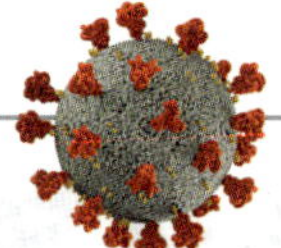

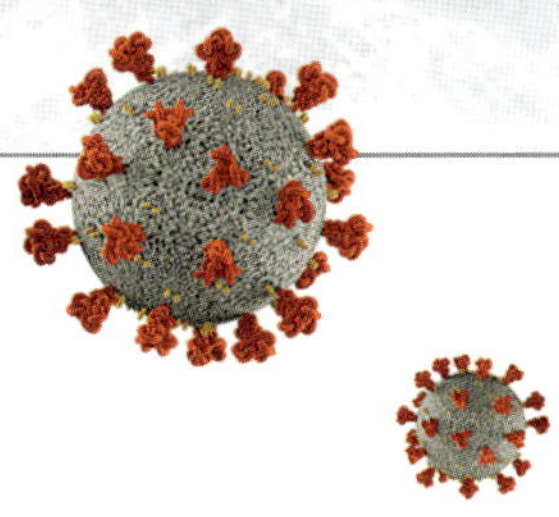

immune response

How the body recognizes and defends itself against bacteria, viruses, and other foreign substances.

lymphocyte

A type of white blood cell that is involved in the body's immune response to detect and destroy outside invaders.

novel

New; never before seen.

pathogen

A bacterium, virus, or other microorganism that can cause disease.

plasma

The clear, yellow liquid part of the blood.

replicate

To create a copy.

variant

A genome of a virus that may contain one or more mutations.

white blood cell

A cell in the blood that is part of the body's immune system, helping fight infection and disease.

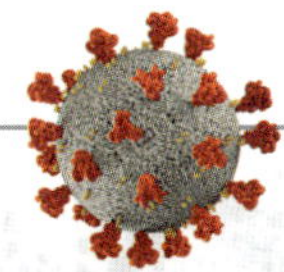

ADDITIONAL RESOURCES

SELECTED BIBLIOGRAPHY

Anthes, Emily. "What the Future May Hold for the Coronavirus and Us." *New York Times*, 12 Oct. 2021, nytimes.com. Accessed 17 Jan. 2022.

Ball, Philip. "The Lightning-Fast Quest for COVID Vaccines—and What It Means for Other Diseases." *Nature*, 18 Dec. 2020, nature.com. Accessed 17 Jan. 2022.

Zuckerman, Gregory. *A Shot to Save the World: The Inside Story of the Life-or-Death Race for a Covid-19 Vaccine.* Portfolio, 2021.

FURTHER READINGS

Blohm, Craig E. *The Search for a COVID-19 Vaccine.* ReferencePoint, 2021.

Deal, Heidi. *Fighting COVID-19 in the United States.* Abdo, 2023.

Edwards, Sue Bradford. *Coronavirus: The COVID-19 Pandemic.* Abdo, 2021.

ONLINE RESOURCES

To learn more about COVID-19 vaccines and treatments, please visit **abdobooklinks.com** or scan this QR code. These links are routinely monitored and updated to provide the most current information available.

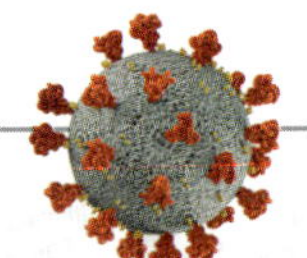

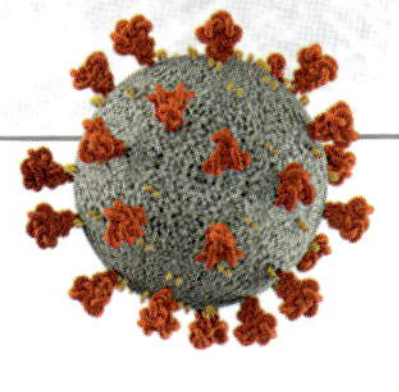

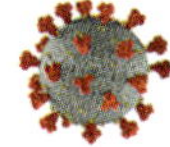

MORE INFORMATION

For more information on this subject, contact or visit the following organizations:

CENTERS FOR DISEASE CONTROL AND PREVENTION (CDC)

1600 Clifton Rd.
Atlanta, GA 30329
1-800-232-4636
cdc.gov

The CDC is the premier public health agency in the United States. It has focused on learning about COVID-19, how it spreads, and how it affects people. The CDC provides the latest guidance on vaccines and treatments to protect the public from COVID-19 and save lives.

US FOOD AND DRUG ADMINISTRATION (FDA)

10903 New Hampshire Ave.
Silver Spring, MD 20993-0002
1-888-463-6332
fda.gov

The FDA is a federal agency in the US Department of Health and Human Services. It is responsible for protecting public health by ensuring the safety of the US food supply, cosmetics, drugs, and other products. The FDA approves all vaccines and treatments, including those for COVID-19, for use in the United States.

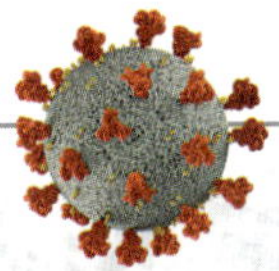

SOURCE NOTES

CHAPTER 1. A SHOT HEARD AROUND THE WORLD

1. "Pfizer and BioNTech Announce Vaccine Candidate against COVID-19 Achieved Success in First Interim Analysis from Phase 3 Study." *Pfizer*, 9 Nov. 2020, pfizer.com. Accessed 18 Mar. 2022.

2. "FDA Takes Key Action in Fight Against COVID-19 by Issuing Emergency Use Authorization for First COVID-19 Vaccine." *FDA*, 11 Dec. 2020, fda.gov. Accessed 18 Mar. 2022.

3. Sharon Otterman. "'I Trust Science,' Says Nurse Who Is First to Get Vaccine in US." *New York Times*, 14 Dec. 2020, nytimes.com. Accessed 18 Mar. 2022.

4. "The Race to Develop a Vaccine for COVID-19." *Cedars Sinai*, 18 May 2020, cedars-sinai.org. Accessed 18 Mar. 2022.

5. Otterman, "'I Trust Science.'"

6. "Coronavirus Resource Center." *Johns Hopkins University of Medicine*, n.d., coronavirus.jhu.edu. Accessed 18 Mar. 2022.

7. "History of 1918 Flu Pandemic." *CDC*, 21 Mar. 2018, cdc.gov. Accessed 18 Mar. 2022.

CHAPTER 2. A HIGHLY CONTAGIOUS VIRUS

1. "WHO Statement Regarding Cluster of Pneumonia Cases in Wuhan, China." *WHO*, 9 Jan. 2020. Accessed 18 Mar. 2022.

2. "Update: Severe Acute Respiratory Syndrome—Worldwide and United States, 2003." *CDC*, 18 July 2003, cdc.gov. Accessed 18 Mar. 2022.

3. "About MERS." *CDC*, 2 Aug. 2019, cdc.gov. Accessed 18 Mar. 2022.

4. Berkeley Lovelace Jr. and Will Feuer. "Doctor Who Treated First US Coronavirus Patient Says COVID-19 Has Been 'Circulating Unchecked' for Weeks." *CNBC*, 6 Mar. 2020, cnbc.com. Accessed 18 Mar. 2022.

5. Lidia Morawska and Donald K. Milton. "It Is Time to Address Airborne Transmission of Coronavirus Disease 2019 (COVID-19)." *Clinical Infectious Diseases*, vol. 71, no. 9, 1 Nov. 2020, pp. 2311–2313, academic.oup.com. Accessed 18 Mar. 2022.

6. "COVID-19 Can Wreck Your Body, Here's How." *Nebraska Medicine*, 7 July 2020, nebraskamed.com. Accessed 18 Mar. 2022.

7. "COVID-19 Can Wreck Your Body."

CHAPTER 3. TREATING COVID-19

1. Kelly Servick, Jennifer Couzin-Frankel, Catherine Matacic. "Medicine's Longest Year." *Science*, 16 Mar. 2021, science.org. Accessed 18 Mar. 2022.

2. Will Feuer. "'Helpless' Doctors at Start of Coronavirus Pandemic Now Have More Treatments to Save Lives." *CNBC*, 29 Sept. 2020, cnbc.com. Accessed 18 Mar. 2022.

3. Servick, "Medicine's Longest Year."

4. Brianna McCabe. "What Is Proning and How May It Help COVID-19 Patients?" *Hackensack Meridian Health*, 6 May 2020, hackensackmeridianhealth.org. Accessed 18 Mar. 2022.

5. Servick, "Medicine's Longest Year."

6. "COVID-19: Who's at Higher Risk of Serious Symptoms?" *Mayo Clinic*, 1 Mar. 2022, mayoclinic.org. Accessed 18 Mar. 2022.

7. Heidi Ledford. "COVID Antibody Treatments Show Promise for Preventing Severe Disease." *Nature*, 12 Mar. 2021, nature.com. Accessed 18 Mar. 2022.

8. Servick, "Medicine's Longest Year."

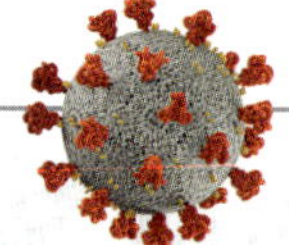

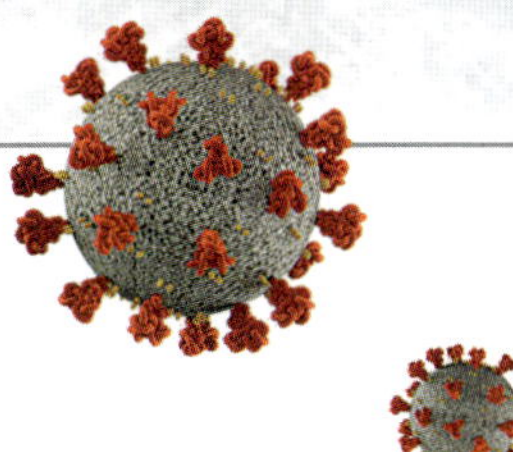

9. Rebecca Robbins. "Pfizer Says Its Antiviral Pill Is Highly Effective in Treating Covid." *New York Times*, 5 Nov. 2021, nytimes.com. Accessed 18 Mar. 2022.

10. Robbins, "Pfizer Says Its Antiviral Pill Is Highly Effective."

11. "Reflecting on Treating the First Person Diagnosed with COVID-19 in the United States." *Stories @ Gilead*, 29 June 2021, stories.gilead.com. Accessed 18 Mar. 2022.

12. Ninh T. Nguyen, Justine Chinn, Jeffry Nahmias. "Outcomes and Mortality Among Adults Hospitalized With COVID-19 at US Medical Centers." *JAMA Network Open*, vol. 4, no. 3, 2021, jamanetwork.com. Accessed 18 Mar. 2022.

CHAPTER 4. VACCINE RESEARCH

1. "Initial Trial of Moderna's COVID-19 Vaccine Began One Year Ago." *WCVB*, 16 Mar. 2021, wcvb.com. Accessed 18 Mar. 2022.

2. Mary Van Beusekom. "Hopeful Results from Phase 1 Moderna COVID Vaccine Trial." *University of Minnesota CIDRAP*, 15 July 2020, cidrap.umn.edu. Accessed 18 Mar. 2022.

3. David Heath and Gus Garcia-Roberts. "Luck, Foresight and Science: How an Unheralded Team Developed a COVID-19 Vaccine in Record Time." *USA Today News*, 26 Jan. 2021, usatoday.com. Accessed 18 Mar. 2022.

4. "Moderna's Fully Enrolled Phase 3 COVE Study of mRNA-1273." *Moderna*, 2021, modernatx.com. Accessed 18 Mar. 2022.

5. Elizabeth Cohen, John Bonifield, and Jamie Gumbrecht. "First Phase 3 Clinical Trial of a Coronavirus Vaccine in the United States Begins." *CNN Health*, 27 July 2020, cnn.com. Accessed 18 Mar. 2022.

6. Philip Ball. "The Lightning-Fast Quest for COVID Vaccines—And What It Means for Other Diseases." *Nature*, 18 Dec. 2020, nature.com. Accessed 18 Mar. 2022.

7. "Pfizer and BioNTech Announce Vaccine Candidate Against COVID-19 Achieved Success in First Interim Analysis from Phase 3 Study." *Pfizer*, 9 Nov. 2020, pfizer.com. Accessed 18 Mar. 2022.

8. "Explaining Operation Warp Speed." *US Department of Health and Human Services*, n.d., nihb.org. Accessed 18 Mar. 2022.

CHAPTER 5. HOW DO THE VACCINES WORK?

1. "COVID-19 Natural Immunity Versus Vaccination." *Nebraska Medicine*, 20 Sept. 2021, nebraskamed.com. Accessed 18 Mar. 2022.

2. Shana Miles. "How Do We Know the COVID-19 Vaccines Are Safe and Effective? One Expert Explains." *American College of Obstetricians and Gynecologists*, Dec. 2020, acog.org. Accessed 18 Mar. 2022.

3. Charlotte Bermingham, Jasper Morgan, Vahé Nafilyan. "Deaths Involving COVID-19 by Vaccination Status, England: Deaths Occurring between 2 January and 2 July 2021." *Office for National Statistics*, 13 Sept. 2021, ons.gov.uk. Accessed 18 Mar. 2022.

CHAPTER 6. VACCINATION CAMPAIGNS

1. Noah Higgins-Dunn and Will Feuer. "'All I Did Was Cry:' Elderly Americans Struggle to Set Up Covid Vaccine Appointments." *CNBC*, 3 Feb. 2021, cnbc.com. Accessed 18 Mar. 2022.

2. Marygrace Taylor. "Relieved, Empowered, Teary-Eyed: 10 People on How They Felt After Their COVID-19 Vaccine." *Prevention*, 12 May 2021, prevention.com. Accessed 18 Mar. 2022.

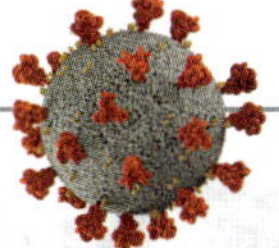

SOURCE NOTES CONTINUED

3. Elizabeth Cohen. "HHS Vaccination Ads Use a New Tactic to Increase COVID-19 Vaccination Rates: Fear." *CNN Health*, 6 Oct. 2021, cnn.com. Accessed 18 Mar. 2022.

4. Cohen, "HHS Vaccination Ads Use a New Tactic."

5. Clara Longo de Freitas. "Hyattsville Barbershop Holds COVID-19 Vaccine Clinic with UMD, Luminis Health Partnership." *Diamondback*, 18 May 2021, dbknews.com. Accessed 18 Mar. 2022.

6. Cecelia Smith-Schoenwalder. "Biden Reaches Goal of 70% of Adults Partially Vaccinated Against COVID-19 a Month Late." *US News & World Report*, 2 Aug. 2021, usnews.com. Accessed 18 Mar. 2022.

7. "Share of People Who Completed the Initial COVID-10 Vaccination Protocol." *Our World In Data*, 18 Mar. 2022, ourworldindata.org. Accessed 18 Mar. 2022.

8. Joe Murphy. "Biden Has New Vaccination Goals. See If the Country Is on Pace to Hit Them." *NBC News*, 27 May 2021, nbcnews.com. Accessed 18 Mar. 2022.

9. Berkeley Lovelace Jr. and Nate Rattner. "US Reaches 70% COVID Vaccine Milestone for Adults About a Month behind Biden's Goal." *CNBC*, 2 Aug. 2021, cnbc.com. Accessed 18 Mar. 2022.

10. Jacob Knutson. "States Deploy Carrots to Drive Up Coronavirus Vaccination Rates." *Axios*, 30 May 2021, axios.com. Accessed 18 Mar. 2022.

11. Linda Geddes. "How Effective Are COVID-19 Vaccines in the Real World?" *Gavi the Vaccine Alliance*, 23 July 2021, gavi.org. Accessed 18 Mar. 2022.

12. Lena H. Sun. "Pfizer, Moderna Vaccines Are 90% Effective after Two Doses in Study of Real-Life Conditions, CDC Confirms." *Washington Post*, 29 Mar. 2021, washingtonpost.com. Accessed 18 Mar. 2022.

13. Sun, "Pfizer, Moderna Vaccines Are 90% Effective."

14. Jason Murdock. "Fauci Tells Zuckerberg COVID Pandemic Won't End Unless 'Overwhelming Majority' Get Vaccinated." *Newsweek*, 1 Dec. 2020, newsweek.com. Accessed 18 Mar. 2022.

CHAPTER 7. VACCINE HESITANCY AND MANDATES

1. Emmarie Huetteman. "Covid Vaccine Hesitancy Drops Among All Americans, New Survey Shows." *Kaiser Family Foundation*, 30 Mar. 2021, khn.org. Accessed 18 Mar. 2022.

2. Edward Chen. "Vaccine Hesitancy: More Than a Pandemic." *Science in the News*, 29 June 2021, sitn.hms.harvard.edu. Accessed 18 Mar. 2022.

3. William A. Galston. "For COVID-19 Vaccinations, Party Affiliation Matters More Than Race and Ethnicity." *Brookings*, 1 Oct. 2021, brookings.edu. Accessed 18 Mar. 2022.

4. Julie Bosman, Jan Hoffman, Margot Sanger-Katz, and Tim Arango. "Who Are the Unvaccinated in America? There's No One Answer." *New York Times*, 31 July 2021, nytimes.com. Accessed 18 Mar. 2022.

5. Megan Lowry and Dara Shefska. "Fighting Vaccine Hesitancy: What Can We Learn From Social Science?" *National Academies of Sciences, Engineering, Medicine*, 1 July 2021, nationalacademies.org. Accessed 18 Mar. 2022.

6. Sara Berg. "What Doctors Wish Patients Knew About COVID-19 Herd Immunity." *American Medical Association*, 27 Aug. 2021, ama-assn.org. Accessed 18 Mar. 2022.

7. Bosman, et al, "Who Are the Unvaccinated?"

8. "FDA Approves First COVID-19 Vaccine." *FDA*, 23 Aug. 2021, fda.gov. Accessed 18 Mar. 2022.

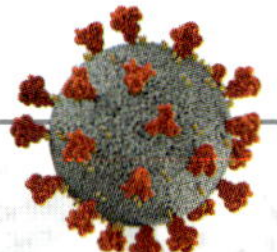

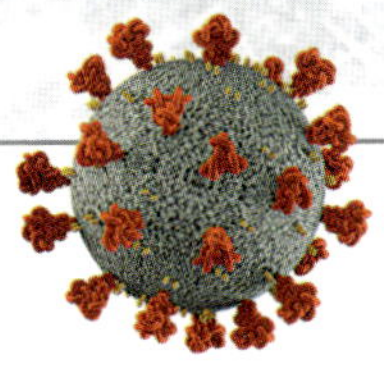

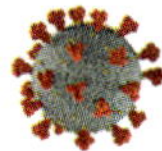

9. Gloria Oladipo. "Unvaccinated Could Be Breeding Ground for COVID Variants, US Officials Fear." *Guardian*, 17 July 2021, theguardian.com. Accessed 18 Mar. 2022.

10. Ivan Pereira. "COVID-19 Vaccine Mandates Moving the Needle, Experts Say." *ABC News*, 9 Nov. 2021, abcnews.go.com. Accessed 18 Mar. 2022.

11. "What Is Smallpox?" *CDC*, 7 June 2016, cdc.gov. Accessed 18 Mar. 2022.

12. Emma G. Fitzsimmons and Lola Fadulu. "Bosses and Workers Face NYC's New Reality: Get Vaccinated or Else." *New York Times*, 7 Dec. 2021, nytimes.com. Accessed 18 Mar. 2022.

CHAPTER 8. VARIANTS, DECLINING IMMUNITY, AND BOOSTER CONFUSION

1. Kathy Katella. "Omicron, Delta, Alpha, and More: What To Know About the Coronavirus Variants." *Yale Medicine*, 17 Mar. 2022, yalemedicine.org. Accessed 18 Mar. 2022.

2. Tanya Lewis. "How Dangerous Is the Delta Variant, And Will It Cause a COVID Surge in the US?" *Scientific American*, 29 June 2021, scientificamerican.com. Accessed 18 Mar. 2022.

3. Lewis, "How Dangerous Is the Delta Variant?"

4. Spencer Kimball. "FDA Clears Moderna's and Pfizer's COVID Vaccine Booster Shots for All US Adults." *CNBC*, 19 Nov. 2021, cnbc.com. Accessed 18 Mar. 2022.

5. "CDC Expands Eligibility for COVID-19 Booster Shots to All Adults." *CDC*, 19 Nov. 2021, cdc.gov. Accessed 18 Mar. 2022.

6. Jack Guy and Mostafa Salem. "COVID-19 Vaccine Boosters Are 'Immoral' And 'Unfair' Says WHO Chief." *CNN*, 12 Oct. 2021, cnn.com. Accessed 18 Mar. 2022.

7. Bridget Balch. "The Vaccines and the Variants: Four Keys to Ending the Pandemic." *Association of American Medical Colleges*, 9 June 2021, aamc.org. Accessed 18 Mar. 2022.

8. Josh Holder. "Tracking Coronavirus Vaccinations Around the World." *New York Times*, 18 Mar. 2022, nytimes.com. Accessed 18 Mar. 2022.

9. Carl Zimmer and Andrew Jacobs. "Omicron: What We Know About the New Coronavirus Variant." *New York Times*, 3 Jan. 2022, nytimes.com. Accessed 18 Mar. 2022.

10. Anne Flaherty. "Kids Are Driving up COVID Cases." *ABC News*, 9 Dec. 2021, abcnews.go.com. Accessed 18 Mar. 2022.

CHAPTER 9. THE FUTURE WITH COVID-19

1. Maya Wei-Haas. "Why Some Coronavirus Variants Are More Contagious." *National Geographic*, 27 Jan. 2021, nationalgeographic.com. Accessed 18 Mar. 2022.

2. "Tracking SARS-CoV-2 Variants." *WHO*, 2022, who.int. Accessed 18 Mar. 2022.

3. Emily Anthes. "What the Future May Hold for the Coronavirus and Us." *New York Times*, 12 Oct. 2021, nytimes.com. Accessed 18 Mar. 2022.

4. Anthes, "What the Future May Hold."

5. Anthes, "What the Future May Hold."

6. Anthes, "What the Future May Hold."

7. Nicky Phillips. "The Coronavirus Is Here to Stay—Here's What That Means." *Nature*, 16 Feb. 2021, nature.com. Accessed 18 Mar. 2022.

8. Ewen Callaway. "Beyond Omicron: What's Next for COVID's Viral Evolution." *Nature*, 7 Dec. 2021, nature.com. Accessed 18 Mar. 2022.

9. Cory Stieg. "The COVID Pandemic Could End Next Year, Experts Say." *CNBC*, 9 Dec. 2021, cnbc.com. Accessed 18 Mar. 2022.

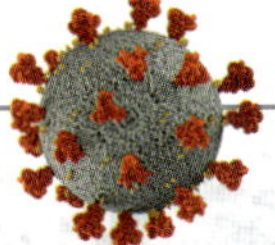

INDEX

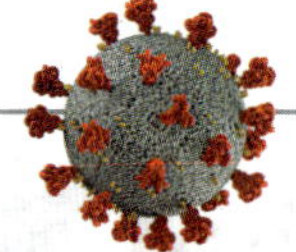

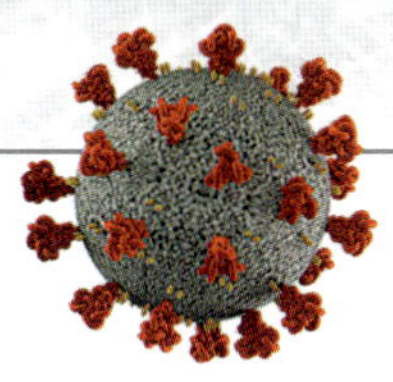

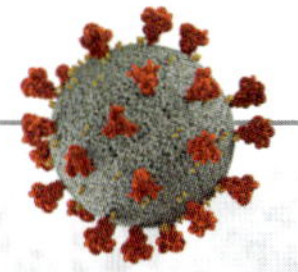

ABOUT THE AUTHOR

CARLA MOONEY

Carla Mooney is a graduate of the University of Pennsylvania with a degree in economics. Today, she writes for young people and is the author of many books for young adults and children. Mooney enjoys learning about science, medicine, and innovation.

ABOUT THE CONSULTANT

KENNETH A. STAPLEFORD

Dr. Kenneth A. Stapleford joined the New York University Grossman School of Medicine Department of Microbiology as an assistant professor in 2016. He received his bachelor of science in biochemistry from the University of Delaware and his PhD in cellular and molecular biology from the University of Michigan. Following his graduate work, he completed a short postdoctoral term at Yale University before moving on to the Institut Pasteur in Paris, France, for his postdoctoral training in RNA virus biology. Dr. Stapleford's lab is interested in understanding the host-pathogen interactions and molecular details involved in RNA virus replication and transmission.

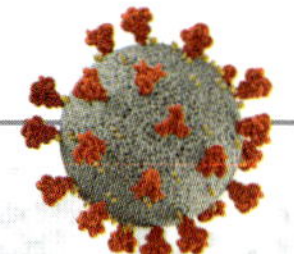